Wars of Scottish Independence

A Captivating Guide to the Battles Between the Kingdom of Scotland and the Kingdom of England, Including the Impact Made by King Robert the Bruce

© Copyright 2018

All Rights Reserved. No part of this book may be reproduced in any form without permission in writing from the author. Reviewers may quote brief passages in reviews.

Disclaimer: No part of this publication may be reproduced or transmitted in any form or by any means, mechanical or electronic, including photocopying or recording, or by any information storage and retrieval system, or transmitted by email without permission in writing from the publisher.

While all attempts have been made to verify the information provided in this publication, neither the author nor the publisher assumes any responsibility for errors, omissions or contrary interpretations of the subject matter herein.

This book is for entertainment purposes only. The views expressed are those of the author alone, and should not be taken as expert instruction or commands. The reader is responsible for his or her own actions.

Adherence to all applicable laws and regulations, including international, federal, state and local laws governing professional licensing, business practices, advertising and all other aspects of doing business in the US, Canada, UK or any other jurisdiction is the sole responsibility of the purchaser or reader.

Neither the author nor the publisher assumes any responsibility or liability whatsoever on the behalf of the purchaser or reader of these materials. Any perceived slight of any individual or organization is purely unintentional.

Free Bonus from Captivating History (Available for a Limited time)

Hi History Lovers!

Now you have a chance to join our exclusive history list so you can get your first history ebook for free as well as discounts and a potential to get more history books for free! Simply visit the link below to join.

Captivatinghistory.com/ebook

Also, make sure to follow us on:

Twitter: @Captivhistory

Facebook: Captivating History:@captivatinghistory

Contents

FREE BONUS FROM CAPTIVATING HISTORY (AVAILABLE FOR A LIMITED TIME) 5

INTRODUCTION 1

CHAPTER 1 – GOOD FENCES; GOOD NEIGHBORS 7

CHAPTER 2 – CRISIS 11

CHAPTER 3 – DEFIANCE 16

CHAPTER 4 – THE MARTYR 23

CHAPTER 5 – POWER STRUGGLES 41

CHAPTER 6 – INNER STRIFE 45

CHAPTER 7 – THE BATTLE OF BANNOCKBURN 50

CHAPTER 8 – A WORTHY KING 55

CHAPTER 9 – WHERE YOUR HEART IS 60

CHAPTER 10 – THE SON OF THE BRUCE & THE SECOND WAR FOR INDEPENDENCE 62

CONCLUSION 74

Introduction

The Scottish independence referendum in 2014 was but one critical episode in the long and complex relationship between Scotland and England. (55.3% of those who voted during the 2014 referendum opined that Scotland should not be an independent country). There has always been a divide between Scotland and its historically wealthier and more powerful southern neighbor. Despite England's longstanding threat of dominance, Scotland had maintained a vigorous and distinctive national culture throughout most of its history. To counter Anglo-Saxon influences in its courts, clergy, culture, and social institutions, Scotland had constantly drawn from the mainstream cultures of Europe (e.g. France and Norway). Its universities have traditionally been open to foreign students and faculty, allowing the educated Scottish classes a measure of cosmopolitanism that was not filtered through an English worldview.

The borderland between Scotland and England has historically been a site of struggle, violence, and conflict. This was acutely so during the First Scottish War of Independence, which lasted from 26 March 1296 – 1 May 1328. (The term "war of independence" was accorded to the period in retrospect after the American War of Independence popularized it, but the spirit was certainly there during the time). The tumult during this medieval period was grand, presenting a historical stage filled with memorable larger-than-life figures: Edward I, an expansionist English monarch who was also known as "Longshanks" and the "hammer of the Scots"; William Wallace also known as

"Braveheart" – a Scottish national symbol par excellence; and Robert de Bruce – Wallace's unlikely spiritual successor and the man who eventually liberated the nation.

The sequence of events that constituted the First Scottish War of Independence was marked by political opportunism at nearly every turn. Before the Scots were embroiled in a bitter conflict that would span over three decades, they were enjoying a "golden age" of peace and prosperity. King Alexander III had been in power since 1249, overseeing an era characterized by awe-inducing architectural accomplishments (monasteries, abbeys, and cathedrals), the flourishing of castles and stately homes, and healthy levels of trading activity with Germany and Scandinavia. Scottish farmers surpassed their English counterparts in terms of their production of wool and cattle. Scotland was then home to nearly half a million people (while England had approximately 2 million). They enjoyed low taxes, access to plentiful food and wine, and a good transportation network. With a firm understanding of the borderline between the two nations in place, life could go on without the distractions of territorial disputes and power struggles.

Royal deaths on both sides of the border changed this state of affairs. King Henry III of England passed away in 1272, and was replaced by his son Edward I: an ambitious ruler with a lifelong attraction to military affairs.[i] After suppressing two rebellions in Wales and subjecting it to English rule, he unveiled similar designs for Scotland. His vision of a Scottish conquest was made possible by King Alexander III's death (from a horse-riding accident) in 1286. Edward took full advantage of the succession crisis that followed to assert himself as a feudal overlord.

The Scottish nobility was divided by a feud between the two leading contenders for the throne: Robert the Bruce and John de Balliol. After being asked by the Guardians of Scotland to judge the contest between them (to avoid a disastrous civil war between the supporters of both clans), he supported Balliol after successfully convincing both prospective kings to swear an oath of fealty to England. Once

Balliol was crowned in 1292, he sought to resist Edward's attempts to overrule and override his powers. (Edward began intervening in Scottish legal cases, claiming taxes, and commanding Balliol to send Scottish soldiers to fight England's battles in France). Between 1296 and 1328, the Scots declared their independence from England and signed an alliance with France. Edward met their refusals and resistance with an outright military invasion, which catalyzed a war that would last for 32 years.

If Edward was expecting his conquest of Wales to repeat itself in Scotland, he was sorely mistaken. The bloody massacre of Berwick (an economically prominent Scottish border-town) and the defeat of the Scottish army were only able to temporarily subdue the Scottish people. The Scottish nobility may have acquiesced themselves to English rule to maintain their lands and wealth in England, but the common people were not so easily cowed. Balliol was imprisoned in London for resisting English rule, but William Wallace eventually rose from anonymity to become a national icon. His army of rebels stood up to the English armed forces – then the most advanced military force in all of Europe – with guerrilla tactics, a shrewd understanding of how to use the Scottish terrain to their own advantage, and an unwavering spirit. Wallace was able to secure an astounding victory over the English army at the Battle of Stirling Bridge in 1298, effectively destroying the English army's reputation of invincibility. Wallace and his men had been armed with spears alone, but they had managed to defeat a much larger force of heavily armed knights and infantrymen. This was Scotland's first military victory against England in centuries.

Wallace's success and position as the Guardian of Scotland would prove to be short-lived, however. His infantrymen were annihilated at the Battle of Falkirk,[ii] where they were pitted against a deadly surprise: the revolutionary range of the English longbow.[iii] Wallace resigned from his position and disappeared into the wilderness once again, but the flames of resistance that his military leadership had ignited burned on. The Scottish resistance fighters continued to deploy his guerrilla tactics against the English army over the next six years (Edward led his army northward each year, before eventually retreating due to fatigue and food shortages).

Unable to defeat England on the battlefield, Scottish resistance leaders turned to diplomacy. The Scottish Church and Wallace attempted to appeal to Phillip IV of France and the papacy to support Scotland's right to independence. Their attempts were compromised by the resurgence of an internal division between the Comyns (who supported Balliol's return as the rightful king of Scotland) and the Bruces (who were against the idea of Balliol's return). The Bruces eventually submitted to Edward I, and support from the papacy did not materialize when the Pope[iv] concluded that Edward's support in his Crusade against Islam was more important than Scottish sovereignty. In 1304, the Scottish nobility finally admitted diplomatic defeat and capitulated to Edward. Wallace was tried as a traitor and publicly – and gruesomely – executed in London to discourage other potential freedom fighters.

Wallace's execution may have appeared to mark the end of an era, but it turned out that the spirit of defiance he had embodied all his adult life survived. Edward's assumption that he had a firm control over Scotland soon proved illusory. Under the pretense of subservience, Robert Bruce, the young Earl of Carrick, made a covert agreement with Bishop Robert Wishart to instigate another uprising. Bruce had his own designs on the Scottish throne; John "The Red" Comyn, the head of the Comyn family and his primary rival for the throne was killed in a church in 1306.[v] Six weeks after the fatal stabbing of "The Red", Bruce was crowned King of Scotland at Scone.

Bruce's moment of glory was initially short-lived. He had initiated a civil war against the Comyns and their supporters, as well as triggered Edward's wrath. After his defeat of the English army at the Battle of Methven in June 1306, he was forced to flee to the Gaelic west. Upon realizing that he stood little chance of success in an open confrontation against the English army's superior numbers and technology, he embarked on a Wallace-like guerrilla campaign against Edward and his other enemies in Scotland. The next year, the tables were turned. Edward died on his way north to battle Bruce, after ordering his men to not bury him properly until the Scots were utterly conquered. As a result, he was entombed in a plain lead casket in Westminster Abbey to this day.

Bruce secured wider support after Edward I's death, and regained control of most of Scotland through military exertion by 1313. He was finally in a position to pacify Balliol's remaining supporters. They were issued an ultimatum: support him or relinquish ownership of all their estates. A more unified Scotland could then turn to face Edward's replacement: his son, Edward II.[vi] The David-versus-Goliath dynamic at the Battle of Stirling Bridge[vii] repeated itself at the Battle of Bannockburn, where the Scottish resistance confronted an English army that was overwhelming in numbers (over 15,000 men) and weaponry.[viii] This victory proved to be Bruce's most prized accomplishment – and a severe humiliation for Edward II.

This military victory elevated Bruce to the position of the rightful King of Scotland in the eyes of his countrymen, but he still had not gained the recognition from England and the papacy. Since Edward II had retreated to York, Bruce was free to invade northern England and Ireland (he proclaimed his intentions to also free the Irish from English subjugation). Meanwhile, he also worked on the diplomatic front to convince the Pope to accept the Declaration of Arbroath (a statement of Scottish independence that would go on to amass great fame) – but was unsuccessful.

Meanwhile, Edward II was losing favor in the eyes of the English nobility and common people. In 1328, he was deposed and murdered. As England was embroiled in a civil crisis, Bruce made a strategic intervention (a historical irony, given the circumstances of Edward I's interventions after Alexander III's untimely death). He launched a successful invasion of Northern England, and threatened to annex the territory he had conquered to Scotland. Edward III was thus prompted to finally recognize that Bruce was the rightful King of Scotland – and that Scotland was an independent nation. After the Treaty of Edinburgh-Northampton was signed on 1 May 1328, plans were made for Robert's son and heir David to be married to Joan of the Tower, Edward III's sister. The first war of Scottish independence had finally ended. Bruce returned home with a place in history, and then died one year later due to illness.

Chapter 1 – Good Fences; Good Neighbors

The modern nation-state is by no means a universally applicable historical phenomenon; the Scotland of the 1200s had only recently arrived at a sense of a national identity. Alexander III,[ix] who was the King of Scotland from 1249 to 1286, oversaw the policies that he had inherited from his predecessors. He relied mostly on a baronage system of Norman origins, which was conducted in French. (The Scots had embraced the fashions of European courts to gain more international clout and full acceptance within the community of West European monarchs).

The Scottish people lived a peaceful and prosperous existence under the same monarch for nearly four generations (who was lauded for governing "in love and law"), with a worldview more centered on local and regional loyalties than a sense of patriotism or nationalism. The term *Scotia*[x] was only applied to the entire kingdom north of England during Alexander II's reign (it had previously only referred to the lands north of the Clyde and Forth isthmus). The idea of "Scottishness" – like the ideas of Englishness, Irishness, and Welshness – is a relatively recent phenomenon. The boundaries between these four different bodies were not always clearly delineated.[xi] In the past, parts of Scotland were ruled from Ireland, England, and Scandinavia, while parts of England and Ireland were ruled from Scotland.

The multiculturalism and multilingualism of Alexander III's diverse dominions reflected the psychical obstacles that stood in the way of a common sense of national belonging. Orkney and Shetland were constituents of the Scandinavian empire. The Inner and Outer Hebrides only entered the domain in 1266. Caithness and Sutherland were predominantly Norse; major parts of the north and west and Galloway (which was in the extreme south-west) were Celtic. Gaelic was still widely spoken in the Lowland counties of Ayr and Lanark. During this time, the Scottish language was slowly gaining eminence across the Lowlands. It originated in the south-east (from the Lothians and around Edinburgh), and would spread northward and westward throughout the twelfth century. It headed in multiple directions, on its way to becoming the lingua franca of Scotland: across the Forth and Clyde basins, westward to Kyle, southward to the Solway, and northward, past the Forth.

Berwick[xii] may pale in comparison to Glasgow[xiii] and Edinburgh[xiv] (the state capital, now and then) today, but it was the most prosperous town and the center of Scottish trade with the Baltic and the Low Countries at the time. (Scotland conducted far less trade with England than it did with northern Germany and Scandinavia). Berwick was compared to Alexandria for its large population and immense wealth; its annual customs revenue was estimated to amount to one-quarter of England's. The stereotype of the Scottish as a "barbaric" and largely tribal people persists today, but the rule of David I[xv] had "tamed" the wild nature of the Gaelic-Norse tribes and introduced the genteel influence of Christianity to the realm. The commissioning of majestic abbeys, monasteries, and churches reflect the growing eminence of the Scottish Church throughout this time. Under his just governance, people with different languages and customs were able to live together in peace and harmony.

The birth of the modern West European state occurred between the twelfth and thirteenth centuries. It was characterized by fully institutionalized administrative and legal systems, representation in parliament, a clearly defined national sovereignty, a commercialized economy, and a common vision of nationhood.[xvi] By 1100, England had developed all of these characteristics under its new Norman rulers and emerged as the most powerful political force in the British Isles. Wales and Ireland were the first political entities to feel the weight of its influence and power. Scotland's ability to defend itself against repeated English attempts to remove its sovereign identity prevented the vision of a fully English kingdom across the entirety of the medieval British Isles to be accomplished.

Scotland's ability to resist English conquest can be attributed to how it was able to absorb novel influences, technologies, and ideas and reshaped them for its own purposes. Scotland was open to colonists from England, Normandy, Brittany, and Flanders, thus exposing itself to the same ideas and political, religious and socio-economic changes that had brought about the "Europeanization of Europe."[xvii] After 1100, nearly every single important development in Scotland was derived from modes and resources that had been established beyond its own borders.

Despite its peaceful coexistence with England up until Alexander III's death, Scotland had been victimized by England's expansionist ambitions. The borders between the two kingdoms had been clearly defined. Scottish kings had long harbored the desire to reclaim Cumbria and Westmorland, which had once belonged to the southern portions of the kingdom of Strathclyde and the old kingdom of Northumbria. The position of Scotland in relation to England had been nebulous since the tenth century, when Scotland had relied on English aid to oppose the Danes. The English ruler had then been defined as "father and lord" of the King of Scots.

This led to an ironic and complicated reality where Scottish kings were also English magnates that owned titles and estates in England (often due to cross-border marriages). Since William the Conqueror[xviii] ruled Scotland, Scottish kings had to do homage for the English fiefs they held. The act of homage was never precisely defined – it involved a ceremony that was performed for the granting of land. This ceremony represented the submission of a vassal to his lord (which had to be there in person). The vassal would remove his crown or helmet, put aside his swords and spurs, and kneel before his lord. He would then stretch out his hands, which the lord would grasp. He would then proclaim: "I become your man from this day forth, of life and limb, and will hold faith to you for the lands I hold." After the act of homage and the oath of fealty, the lord and vassal would partake in the ceremony of investiture. The obligations that accompanied the act of homage were not explicitly stated, but they served as a powerful moral sanction for more specific responsibilities and engagements.

The Treaty of Falaise[xix] in 1174 provides a sense of the relative positions of both Kingdoms. William the Lion had been captured by the English army, and would only be released if he agreed to pay homage to Henry for the Scottish crown. These terms were nevertheless cancelled after fifteen years, when Richard the Lionheart[xx] decided to sell the rights that his father had acquired to pay for his ventures in the Holy Land. This new agreement annulled the Treaty of Falaise, leaving the implications of homage as open-ended as it had been prior to 1174.

One of David I's legacies included the institutionalization of a strict form of kingship that depended on royal succession. This perpetuated a national monarchy and saved Scotland from the disruptions and costs of prolonged competitions for the throne. Alexander III thus succeeded the throne as a 7-year old in 1249 without any contestation. His long reign rested on the presumption that the Scottish kingship was equal in power and sovereignty to the English kingship; the Scottish kings also sought to obtain the pope's approval of the Scottish crown as a God-ordained anointment. In 1278, Alexander III was pressured to subject himself to Edward I. He confidently declined: "No one has the right to homage for my kingdom save God alone."

Chapter 2 – Crisis

As King Alexander III's long reign drew towards an end, Edward I was wrapping up his conquest of Wales. After six years of battle, he secured a victory in 1283. Two years later, he headed to Paris to pay homage to the new French king, Philip the Fair. [xxi] He remained there for three years, apparently confident of his power over England and Wales. While he was away, many prominent English ministers and judges became impossibly corrupt. Edward I was forced to return in 1289, and he decided to use the Jews as a scapegoat for the economic tumult and political chaos of the time. They were all expelled from England (a dangerous precedent for the rest of Europe), but all of their property and wealth remained, to be absorbed by the English state. Now flush with funding, Edward turned his expansionist gaze towards Scotland.

If Alexander III had heeded the prophecy of Thomas the Rhymer[xxii] (Sir Thomas Rymour of Ercildoune), there would have been an entirely different history written. The soothsayer had already predicted his imminent death, but Alexander decided to make the ill-advised decision to ride home during a storm at night. On 18 March 1286, he was attending a council in Edinburgh Castle. Instead of spending the night there after enjoying a good meal and fine wine with his barons, he decided to head home that night. This was presumably motivated by love or lust for his young French wife, Joleta of Dreux. At twenty-two, she was half his age. Alexander III had recently remarried after his first wife, Princess Margaret of

England, died in 1275. The entire kingdom had been hoping for news of a healthy male heir. (Alexander's two sons had died before him, in 1281 and 1284).

Instead, everyone mourned when they heard that the king had been found dead, at the rocks at the foot of the cliffs. In the darkness and deafening howl of the winds, he had been separated from his two local guides and three esquires. The only surviving offspring was his granddaughter, Margaret of Norway.[xxiii] Her mother had died during childbirth, leaving her under the care of her husband, King Eric II of Norway. [xxiv] Two weeks after Alexander's death, Margaret was sworn in as the sovereign lady of Scotland. Six Guardians of Peace were elected as regents: two earls, two barons, and two bishops.

The Guardians of Peace maintained an uneasy peace for the next three years. By then, rivaling powerful factions had appeared, each with their own intentions for the empty throne. On 18 July 1920, the Guardians signed The Treaty of Birgham.[xxv] Its intentions were to maintain the peaceful coexistence between Scotland and England by having Margaret of Norway marry Lord Edward (the then-five-year-old son of King Edward I) when both royal children were of age. The two kingdoms would nevertheless remain separate; Margaret was to be hailed as Scotland's "true lady, queen and heir." In the Treaty, Edward I acknowledged Scotland's identity as a fully developed state that was "distinct and free from the realm of England," with its own "rightful boundaries" and "laws, liberties, and customs."[xxvi] Edward was, however, harboring intentions to exert influence over his northern neighbor through his son's marriage. Everyone's intentions came to nothing, however, when Margaret died due to seasickness while sailing from Norway to Scotland. A direct, uninterrupted lineage of Scottish monarchs had come to a tragic end.

No less than thirteen candidates laid out their claims for the throne, each arguing that they were blood descendants of the Scottish royal family. Since Margaret's mother was dead, Eirik II of Norway no longer had a rightful claim to the throne. After the claims that were based on illegitimate offspring were dismissed, two main candidates for the throne emerged. They were John de Balliol[xxvii] and Robert de Bruce.[xxviii] Both men had large numbers of supporters and armed forces at their command. Scotland was poised to plunge into a disastrous civil war.

The Guardians of Scotland decided to invite Edward to adjudicate both men's claims, on account of his status as the King of England and his renowned legal expertise. Edward had a formidable reputation as an effective king. After he was crowned in 1272, he successfully corrected the legacy of his father, Henry III.[xxix] A reign characterized by internal strife and military impotence gave way to peace and military might. Edward had successfully negotiated peace between the warring English barons and demonstrated his prowess as a leader on the battlefield. He was also an intellectual with novel ideas on how he could successfully reform the English administration and government. Under his oversight, the Parliament maintained stability while collecting copious amounts of taxes from the English population. Whatever they felt towards Edward, the Scots would have to concede that he was a formidable opponent. After he died in 1307, they began referring to him as "Scottorum malleus": the Hammer of the Scots. (His nickname in life was "Longshanks" for his outstanding height).

Instead of concurring with Scotland's understanding of English overlordship as a matter of the distant past, Edward boldly proclaimed his overlordship over Scotland in the presence of the Scottish nobles and clergy on 10 May 1291. He argued that this would justify his appointment as adjudicator of who was the rightful ruler of Scotland. He then gave the Scottish nobles three weeks to put together a rebuttal after they vigorously objected to this shocking plot twist. During this time, he started assembling an army for the highly probability of a military skirmish.

The Scottish nobility were certainly more self-serving than they were patriotic or nationalistic. Many of them owned titles to large swaths of land in England, and were not willing to sacrifice those assets for the sake of national independence. *All* of the competitors for the Scottish throne soon decided to accept Edward's position as Lord Paramount of Scotland. They would agree with his decision on who was the rightful ruler of Scotland. Edward carefully had each competitor write down this acknowledgment and stamp the document with their official seal. He also had every Scottish castle in the kingdom temporarily surrendered to him and replaced all Scottish officials with Englishmen. Every Scottish magnate, knight, freeman, and religious leader had to swear their loyalty to him by 27 July or endure harsh penalties.

John Balliol was eventually crowned King of Scotland in December 1292:

"As it is admitted that the kingdom of Scotland is indivisible, and, as the king of England

must judge of the rights of his subjects according to the laws and usages of the kingdoms

over which he reigns; and as, by the laws and usages of England and Scotland in the

succession to indivisible heritage, the more remote in degree of the first line of descent is

preferable to the nearer in degree of the second line; therefore it is decreed that John

Balliol shall have seisin of the kingdom of Scotland[xxx]."

Edward's decision to favor John Balliol was logical, since he was descended from a royal sister that was older than Robert Bruce's descendant. (Bruce had countered Balliol's claim by noting that he was one less generation removed from the royal lineage. He was the son of David I's great-granddaughter, while Balliol was the grandson of another great-granddaughter). It is nevertheless likely that he also had ulterior motives in favoring Balliol. Since he possessed significant amounts of land in the North of England, he had more to lose from defying Edward. Once Balliol was crowned King of

Scotland, Edward was quick to assert his powers of overlordship. Scotland was now under English occupation in disguise.

The Scottish earls, knights, dukes, and magnates may have consigned themselves to the new status quo to protect their own interests, but the common people had little to gain – and much to lose – from meekly accepting the constant presence of the English military forces in their everyday lives. They were a proud people who felt humiliated by the easy, dishonorable way in which their elites had simply surrendered control of the nation to the English. Incidents of defiance and resistance soon gave way to brawls and riots in various Scottish towns and villages. A knight named Sir Malcolm Wallace died in one such conflict, leaving his son with a deep resentment towards the English that would remain with him until the day he died. His name was William Wallace.[xxxi]

Chapter 3 – Defiance

The exact circumstances of William Wallace's origins are difficult to pin down, but his final resting place – in the hearts and minds of generations of proud Scottish patriots – is well known. Long before the rest of the world became acquainted with the legend of William Wallace via Mel Gibson's 1995 film *Braveheart*[xxxii] (Gibson directed and starred in the Oscar-studded blockbuster), the citizens of Scotland had become familiarized with his outsized accomplishments through the work of fifteenth-century Scottish royal court poet Harry the Minstrel (or "Blind Harry ").[xxxiii] Blind Harry's *The Actes and Deidis of the Illustre and Vallyeant Campioun Schir William Wallace* (Acts and Deeds of the Illustrious and Valiant Champion Sir William Wallace, also known as *The Wallace*) was published nearly two centuries after Wallace's death.[xxxiv] The epic "romantic biographical" poem eventually became the second most popular book in Scotland after the Bible – a position that it retained for hundreds of years.

Before he made the meteoric rise to become a national icon, military legend, and patriot of the highest order, Wallace was the younger son of a minor nobleman. While he was never deprived of food, shelter, or an education, he also had no land titles to his name. Wallace lived his early life in what was termed the Scottish "golden age." Scotland enjoyed low taxes, bridges, good roads, and a thriving agricultural and cattle industry that surpassed even the English at the time.

When King Henry III of England died his son Edward, I took the throne. Edward was to be Wallace's most powerful opponent in the coming decades. While not having the same build as Wallace, Edward was nonetheless also known for his remarkably tall stature and deemed "Long-shanks." Wallace's adult height – a staggering two meters (six foot seven inches), at a time when the average adult man was only slightly taller than five feet – is testament to his exceptional genetics and the prosperity of his era. Blind Harry heaped poetic praise on his physique, singling out his wavy brown locks, sturdy neck, handsome facial features, broad shoulders, piercing eyes, and unmistakable "manly make."

At a time when close combat with sword or dagger were the common methods of physical dominance, Wallace's physical advantage would have served him well. However, without a keen mind to match he would not have reached the heights that made him figure of legend. Historians have speculated that he received an education from the monks in his area, learning to read and write. Wallace was also instructed in the manly arts of warfare, from riding to swordplay. He was trained in the use of a claymore (a two-handed sword) and also a dirk (a long slender dagger used for thrusting). Claymores were prodigious single warrior weapons at the time, taller than most men at six feet in length. Wallace's strength and a six-foot blade were more than enough to cleave through the armor available during his era.

In 1293, when Wallace was between eleven and thirteen years old, Edward I had just concluded his conquest of Wales after a six-year campaign. Edward then traveled to Paris to pay homage to France's new king; Philip the Fair. While away from England, Edward was confident in the knowledge that England and Wales were firmly under his control. Unfortunately, during his absence, many of his ministers and judges would sink to even greater depths of corruption. Edward returned to England in 1289 in the middle of political chaos and economic strife. He decided to expel all Jews from his kingdom, using them as a scapegoat for the current crisis. Once England had settled down, the ambitious leader then turned his gaze towards Scotland.

On 18th March 1286, King Alexander died. After attending a council meeting at Edinburgh Castle he decided to return home, but became separated from his escort and guides. He was found the next day, his dead body recovered from the rocks at the foot of the cliffs. After two weeks of mourning, Alexander's granddaughter, Margaret of Norway, was sworn in as the sovereign lady of Scotland.

Plans were made to marry Margaret of Norway to the son of King Edward I. The Treaty of Birgham was signed on 18 July 1286, effectively uniting the two royal members whilst still keeping England and Scotland separate. It was Edwards's intention to exert his influence on Scotland through his new daughter-in-law, however both his plans and the hopes of Scotland died with Margaret when she succumbed to sickness while at sea while traveling from Norway to Scotland.

Of the thirteen candidates for the throne after Margaret's death, two emerged with serious consideration; John de Balliol and Robert de Bruce. Since each man was backed by their own forces, Scotland appeared to be on the cusp of civil war. In the meantime, Edward, proffering advice and aid during Scotland's succession period, secretly met with his privy council to reveal his plans to subdue Scotland.

Unfortunately for Scotland, Edward I was a supremely able and effective leader. He inherited a throne fraught with internal instability after the passing of his father in 1272, and since his accession he had negotiated peaceful relations between England's restless barons, uniting them under his rule. His methods, while not always considered ethical, were highly effective. His skills also extended to raising funds, encouraging his Parliament to collect large amounts of taxes from the population. In 1275, he imposed the highly popular Statute of the Jewry, forcing exorbitant taxes on the Jewish population of England. By 1290 all Jews were expelled from the country, with all their financial assets confiscated by the crown. His financial prosperity thus positioned him in a favorable condition to begin a campaign north, into the lands of Scotland.

Meanwhile in Scotland, with the two factions of John de Balliol and Robert de Bruce threatening civil war, the guardians of Scotland decided to invite Edward I to adjudicate the many claims to the Scottish throne. On 10 May 1291, King Edward proclaimed his rule over Scotland. In front of an assembly of Scottish nobles and clergy, Edward exerted both his position as an adjudicator and a "legitimate claimant" of the throne. He allowed three weeks for the gathered noblemen to formulate a rebuttal, yet he would use those weeks wisely, marshaling his armies and preparing for military action.

Most of the Scottish noblemen had lands and estates in English territory and knew well that they would be lost should they refuse Edward. All claimants for the throne eventually conceded to Edward's proclamation, naming him as Lord Paramount, accepting his judgment. Edward wasted no time, ordering that every Scottish castle be surrendered to him temporarily, and that all Scottish officials and judges be replaced by Englishmen. All nobility of Scottish descent, including knights, freemen, and religious leaders were to swear to Edward by 27 July or face harsh consequences.

Wallace was on the cusp of manhood (between seventeen to eighteen years old) when his father refused to administer his oath to Edward as Lord Paramount of Scotland. To escape the severe penalties that followed from this decision, he was forced to head northward with his father. His previous plans to embark on a lifelong career as a priest were thus permanently disrupted. While in hiding, his father was embroiled in a sporadic uprising of the Scottish villagers and townspeople against the imperious English soldiers (a fairly common occurrence, since the common people resented their interference in their everyday lives). Sir Malcolm Wallace was killed in one of these riots, leaving behind a son who would always harbor an intractable resentment towards the English.

The specific details may have been lost to time, but it is evident that Wallace's transformation into a feared guerrilla leader began not long after he endured the loss of his father. By 1291, Wallace was actively seeking ways to avenge his father and help his countrymen regain the upper hand against the English. Wallace's first high-profile target was the twenty-year-old son of Selby, an English constable serving under Baron Brian Fitz-Alan of Bedale. In response to the arrogant Englishman's taunts, Wallace stabbed him in the heart and wounded his comrades as he made for a quick escape. His brazen defiance soon earned him notoriety as an outlaw. To get around as a wanted man, he began wearing disguises (e.g. as a pilgrim) and spending more time in the safety of the Scottish woods.

Wallace was not alone in his defiance. King John Balliol resented Edward's interference in the country's national affairs and his status as a puppet figure. Edward had made him repeat his homage several times – a humiliation that was witnessed by the majority of nobles in the land. Edward angered King John further when he began interfering in the decisions made by Scottish courts. He deemed this a violation of the Treaty of Birgham, which mandated that all Scottish lawsuits should be adjudicated in Scotland. Edward then coerced him into acknowledging that the Treaty was now void – which thus established a troubling precedent where anyone could appeal to the English courts when the Scottish courts arrived at an unwanted decision.

King John seized the opportunity to retaliate when Edward got a taste of his own medicine in October 1293. King Philip of France was then in the enviable position of being England's feudal superior. After several English sailors went on an ill-advised rampage at the La Rochelle port, he ordered for all trade between the two countries to be halted. Edward responded by declaring war against France in October the following year. While Adolf of Germany remained neutral, France allied itself with Eirik II of Norway and Florence of Holland. Edward was preoccupied with a rebellion in Wales at the time, and demanded that King John report to London by 1 September 1294 with his armed forces to support him. Instead, King John allied Scotland with France and Norway and openly defied Edward on the 22nd of October.

The Scottish and English forces both prepared for a northern confrontation after Edward ordered for all of King John's titles and properties in England to be seized. The Scots had an early victory at the English town of Carlisle. Since they could not break through its defenses, they burned down the homes of the English citizens who lived outside the town walls. They also pillaged the monasteries, churches and villages in the countryside before returning past the Scottish border.

Edward had Scotland pay a bloody price for these transgressions. Three thousand foot soldiers and five thousand horsemen descended on Berwick, Scotland's largest and most prosperous city at the time. The townspeople were massacred, raped, and burned without mercy and remorse – as an example to the entire Scottish population. Edward only decided to call off the slaughter when he saw one of his soldiers hacking a woman apart as she was giving birth. At least seventeen thousand Scottish townsfolk (Berwick had a population of approximately twenty thousand people) had perished in the process.

The people of Scotland were nevertheless an immensely prideful and hardy group – they were not easily cowed (even by such shocking acts of bloodshed and violence). They rallied behind King John in defying English rule. On the 5th of April, he formally renounced his allegiance to Edward. Scottish renegades pulled off counterattacks to avenge their fallen countrymen at Berwick. After rebuilding Berwick, reinforcing it, and designating it as the new administrative center of his Scottish government, Edward launched his second attack against King John. The English army was then the most formidable military force in Europe, and the Scottish army did not stand a chance in a direct confrontation. Edward imprisoned 130 prominent Scottish knights, alongside a few earls and important magnates. His seamless victory crippled the Scottish victory, allowing the army to capture and seize control of all the major Scottish castles: Roxburgh Castle, Edinburgh Castle, and Stirling Castle. By the 2nd of July, King John had formally surrendered and shipped off to England – where he was placed under a lengthy house arrest.

Before he left, Edward ripped out the royal Scottish insignia from his surcoat. Determined to stamp out all remaining symbols of Scotland's national identity, he also removed the Stone of Destiny (*Lia Fail*). This was the legendary basalt stone where every Celtic Scottish king had been crowned since the sixth century. After he arranged for himself to be crowned on the stone at Scone, he shipped it to Westminster Abbey alongside Scotland's crown jewels. They were only returned to Scotland in 1996. Edward also spirited away three chests that contained decades of royal records and important archives, which were never to be found again.

An all-important parliament session was held at Berwick on 28 August 1296. The agenda of the day was for all of Scotland's important bishops, earls, barons, abbots and priors to pledge their loyalties to him. Edward did not claim the title of King of Scotland for himself, however. Instead, everyone present paid homage to him as the King of England, Lord of Ireland and Duke of Guyenne. With John Balliol out of the picture, Robert Bruce, Lord of Annandale, was hoping to be named as his successor to the Scottish throne. After all, he had allied himself with Edward throughout King John's rule (and brief defection). Having had to exert himself to quash a rebellion, Edward was not interested in enshrining another figurehead. Satisfied with his grip over the country, he left Scotland a mere eleven days after the ceremony. He had to attend to more pressing matters that involved France. The bulk of the English army returned home when winter came, leaving a few garrisons behind to retain control of all of Scotland's castles.

Chapter 4 – The Martyr

Life under English rule was harsh and degrading for the common Scottish people. The English soldiers lorded over all the important Scottish castles and fortresses. They patrolled the countryside each day, ready to flex their military might and superiority complex against any man or woman who was deemed to be lacking in humility and subservience. The just rule of law was suspended in favor of exorbitantly harsh punishments for minor offenses. Scotsmen were flogged, mutilated and hung for mere misdemeanors. The mortality rate in the 1290s was thus exceptionally high.

Without a legitimate legal system in place, many people were forced to take matters into their own hands, some becoming brigands and forming robber bands to exact some measure of justice upon the English soldiers who freely roamed their countryside. English historians were quick to denounce the actions of the Scottish population, lamenting the atrocities committed against English soldiers. Rather hypocritically on the part of the historians, the barbarisms committed by the English soldiers against the Scottish population were not equally subject to condemnation.

Given these circumstances, it is not surprising that news of Wallace's exploits were greeted with much enthusiasm and awe during this time. Blind Harry's epic poem preserves the adulation of Wallace as the equivalent of Nottingham's Robin Hood, a charismatic outlaw that served an inspiring brand of vigilante justice to the English soldiers.

One such instance recorded in Blind Harry's epic poem details a challenge taken up by Wallace which had been put forth by an English soldier/weightlifter in the town of Ayr. Boasting of English superiority, the Soldier challenged any Scotsman to strike him across the back. Wallace, while in disguise, accepted the challenge and broke the English soldier's back with a single blow. He then quickly killed five other English soldiers before making his escape to Leglen Wood.

The Scottish people gained a measure of pride and awe in listening to (and repeating) tales of Wallace's small victories against the hated English. Between 1293, Wallace was transformed from a lone outlaw to a skilled militia leader. His swordsmanship and athletic prowess improved, as did his leadership skills and acumen as a military strategist.

Wallace's reputation also began to take on mythic qualities during his lifetime – a factor that arguably compensated for his lack of wealth and noble standing in the ideas of the common people.[xxxv] In one particular skirmish in the town of Aur, Wallace nearly died after killing one of Lord Percy's men. Unable to escape from the overwhelming number of English soldiers that accosted him, he was captured and starved in a dungeon. When it was time for his trial, a severe fever had put him in a deep coma. The English soldiers assumed that he was dead and left his body to rot in a heap of dung. Wallace would have perished if not for the care and cunning of his first nurse at Ellerslie. She pleaded with the English for a chance to give him a proper burial, and quickly staged a fake wake to keep up the pretense that he was dead when she discovered that he was still alive.

After she nursed him back to health, Wallace gained a Christ-like reputation for having "returned from the dead." His fame grew when Thomas the Rhymer – a renowned prophet and soothsayer who had predicted Alexander III's death – learned that he was miraculously alive and prophesied that he would play a crucial role in restoring Scottish pride:

"For sooth, ere he decease,

Shall many thousands in the field make end.

From Scotland he shall forth the Southron send,

And Scotland thrice he shall bring to peace.

So good of hand again shall ne'er be kenned."[xxxvi]

In an age of superstition and destiny, Wallace had effectively turned into a magnetic larger-than-life figure. Men from all walks of life flocked to his side, turning the lone outlaw into a charismatic militia leader. He inspired faith, loyalty, and devotion in the band of brothers, nephews, uncles, cousins, and distant relatives that formed a tightly-knit military force around him. Motivated by the strength of large numbers, Wallace began to defy Edward's rule more brazenly.

In 1297, Wallace finally seized the opportunity to avenge his father's death. He successfully ambushed Fenwick, the English knight who had killed his father, after learning that he had returned to execute a mission in Scotland. By now, Wallace and his men had the benefit of more sophisticated weaponry: a steel helmet, armor for the torso and hands, a habergeon, and a steel collar. Wallace and his fifty men forced Fenwick – who was accompanied by one hundred and eighty men – to fight them on foot by stabbing the English horses under their bellies. Fenwick and his lieutenants were swiftly butchered, but eighty English soldiers managed to escape. (Wallace only lost three of his men). Wallace's army then claimed two hundred horses and the provisions they were carrying, along with the fallen English knights' weapons, armor, and money.

The news of this victory inspired many Scottish men and fugitives to join Wallace or resist the English in their own way. The English knights' reputation of invincibility had been punctured. Lord Percy initially attempted to establish a truce with Wallace (many Scottish magnates had switched sides after being lured by the promise of large estates and wealth). Wallace's uncle, Sir Ranald Crawford, managed to convince him to accept the truce presented to him.

However, Wallace proved incapable to adapting to a life of peace and quiet after disbanding his army. After a bloody confrontation with English soldiers in town and the murder of several of Lord Percy's own men (they impertinently demanded that Wallace hand over Sir Ranald's pack horse), Wallace was formally declared as an outlaw and an enemy of King Edward.

After recruiting sixty hardened men, Wallace began to emulate Robin Hood. His men began robbing and killing English knights and dispersing their possessions to the Scottish people. They took on Sir James Butler of Kinclaven and his men, once again nullifying the advantage of their horses and superior armor by forcing them to fight on foot. Wallace's victory streak was only disrupted by Sir Gerard Heron's thousand-man cavalry. Wallace's men were formidable in close combat, but they were easy targets for the English archers and their ample supply of arrows. After losing many of his men and suffering an arrow to his own neck (which left a lasting scar), Wallace was forced to retreat.

The most recent and well-known depiction of the tale of William Wallace is found in the 1995 Hollywood blockbuster film Braveheart. In this adaptation of the legend of Wallace, the love interest Murron MacClannough is introduced. Her attempted rape and murder further inspired Wallace to lead a revolt against the English. Although this addition of a lover further endows the tale of William Wallace with poetic justice, the original tale of Wallace by Blind Harry makes no mention of a Murron MacClannough. The original poem does, mention a woman named Innis who was credited with helping him escape from English troops, but there is no indication that she was either his wife or lover.

While the film does draw upon a love story as the initial motivation for Wallace's rebellion, the source is not entirely inaccurate. In a 1570 revised edition of Blind Harry's poem an eighteen-year-old, Marion Braidfute, is introduced as William Wallace's wife. In this edition, the motivations for Wallace's rebellion begin with the murder of Marion by the Sheriff of Lanark.

The poem's plot is simple and symbolic. Wallace meets Marion at an early age, falling in love with her at first sight at the Church of Saint Kentigern, near Lanark. Wallace began seeing Marion in secret, as their love during a time of civil unrest and war was seen as imprudent. To further complicate matters, the Sheriff of Lanark is, at the time, interested in Marion as a potential wife for his son.

The story continues as William Heselrig, Sheriff of Lanark, insults Wallace one Sunday morning as he is leaving Saint Kentigern's Church, leading to a fight between the English soldiers accompanying the Sheriff and Wallace's men. Wallace, having reportedly already married Marion in secret by this time, takes refuge in her home after retreating. A group of English soldiers accompanied by the Sheriff of Lanark marches to Marion's home and demands William's surrender. Marion buys enough time for William to escape out of a back window, however, once the Sheriff realizes that he had been tricked, he storms the home of Marion with his men and murders her in a rage.

Many historians argue that the addition of Marion was a result of a noble family's attempts to claim a link between their ancestry and Wallace's, with Marion having conveniently given birth to a daughter prior to her death at the hands of the Sheriff. The 1570s revision of Blind Harry's poem indicates that Wallace and Marion did manage to marry in secret and produce a daughter prior to her murder. The daughter subsequently married a squire named Shaw, thus preserving Wallace's lineage.

Several historians have dismissed all claims of the existence of Marion, claiming Wallace to have had no heirs, illegitimate or otherwise.

Whether the existence of Marion, or Murron, was fact or fiction, historians do confirm that Wallace successfully murdered the Sheriff of Lanark in May 1297. The night of the supposed murder of Marion, Wallace and his men returned to town, battling their way through the town's defenses and reportedly killing as many as 240

Englishmen. Wallace himself made straight for Heselrig's rooms, finding him and dispatching him with a single cut from his skull right down to the collarbone. After dealing with the Sheriff, he moved on to kill his adult son and then burned the family's house to the ground.

Though the motives may still be questioned, the killing of the Sheriff of Lanark was supported as truth in Wallace's trial documents. His charges at the trial noted the murder of the Sheriff as a symbolic action, one which galvanized the existing various resistance efforts into the first Scottish War of Independence.

After the massacre of Lanark, Wallace rallied his forces in Ayrshire, the territory he was most familiar with. Now in the company of old and new followers who were all under the spell of his revolutionary zeal, he had three thousand well-armed men at his disposal. His ranks included Gilbert de Grimsby (who was widely known as Jop), an esteemed soldier who had served in the English army and gained recognition from King Edward himself. With his formidable experience and critical intelligence regarding the English army, he was made Wallace's standard-bearer immediately. Wallace also had the support of Robert Wishart (the Bishop of Glasgow) and James the Steward, who had both been elected Guardians of Scotland in 1286. Wishart was opposed to Edward's attempts to anglicize the Scottish Church and was happy to support Wallace with his network of like-minded clergymen, the cover of the church, and his ability to "justify" Wallace's revolt as a legitimate war in the name of King John.

Several other prominent Scottish figures also defected to ally themselves with Wallace's brave band of rebels. This included William Douglas "the Bold" and Robert Bruce, the future King of Scotland.[xxxvii] Andrew de Moray, scion of an influential northern family which had led a revolt against the English and united the entire Moray area against them, became another noteworthy ally. Emboldened by Edward's absence (who had placed the ineffectual Hugh Cressingham in charge of English interests in Scotland),

Wallace planned an attack on Perth – the center of the English regime in Scotland. The English were forced to retreat into the castles as the Scottish army advanced, leaving Wallace and his men free to claim the spoils and terrorize the English in turn.

In response, Edward rallied an army of three thousand horsemen and forty thousand footmen. His decisive show of force prompted the Scottish magnates to surrender on the 7th of July, since they were unable to reach a consensus on the army's leadership structure – or to establish an effective chain of command. Wallace was left to attack Lord Percy's forces with the help of Moray and his rebel army. After killing over five hundred English soldiers, they emerged victorious. When August 1297 ended, Wallace had reclaimed a large majority of northern Scotland. Apart from the strongholds of Dundee and Stirling, the English military presence had been purged from the land, forcing Hugh Cressingham to write to Edward informing him that no funding could be taxed from Scotland and requesting further aid from John de Warenne, the Earl of Surrey and Edward's Governor in Scotland:

> *"Sire, at the time when this letter was made, nor previously, from the time when I left you, not a penny could be raised in your [realm of Scotland by any means] until my lord the Earl of Warren shall enter into your land and compel the people of the country by force and sentences of law"*

Edward ordered John de Warenne to provide support to the garrison at Stirling and to raise the siege at Dundee. Wallace was busy attempting to subdue the English forces at Dundee when he learned of a large English force, led by Warenne and Cressingham, moving northward towards Stirling.

Stirling is located in a strategically crucial position in Scotland. The castle itself was perched upon a large crag that overlooked the surrounding plains and was one of the most formidable in the British Isles. Stirling was the gateway to the highlands, and so retaking the castle was seen by the English as the first step in reestablishing control over the north.

Warenne was confident of an English victory, having a vastly superior force and it was assumed that Wallace's rebellion would end with defeat in battle or by negotiation. And yet history would name Stirling as the site of Wallace's most iconic military victory, where he apprehended Cressingham and John de Warenne's large English army.[xxxviii] Despite their vastly superior numbers, weaponry, and logistics, the English cavalry and infantry was fatally undermined by the narrowness of the Stirling Bridge. It was only wide enough to accommodate two horsemen traveling abreast; the 16,000-strong English army would take a few hours to cross over in its entirety, all the while being in a strategically disadvantageous position.

Warrene had expected Wallace and Moray to surrender without a fight and was surprised when the much smaller army set up on the opposing bank, refusing to admit defeat. For a few days, both forces faced one another, each unwilling to make the first move. Warrene sent across the river two Dominican friars to negotiate a surrender. They returned with this message:

> "Tell your commander that we are not here to make peace but to do battle, defend ourselves and liberate our kingdom. Let them come on, and we shall prove this in their very beards."

Overconfident and impatient, because a prolonged battle meant more military expenditures, Warenne finally ordered his troops to cross the bridge on the 11th of September.

The entire English force was to move across the narrow bridge and engage the enemy on the opposite bank. A suggestion was put forth by Richard Lundie, a Scottish noble who had switched allegiance. He urged the English to send a force of horsemen and infantry upstream, to the Ford of Drip, to provide protection to the rest of the army as it advanced across the river:

> "My lords, if we go on to the bridge we are dead men; for we cannot cross it except two by two, and the enemy are on our flank, and can come down on us as they will, all in one front. But there is a ford not far from here, where we can cross sixty at a time. Let me now, therefore, have five hundred knights and a small body of infantry, and we will get around the enemy on the rear and crush them; and meanwhile, you, my Lord Earl, and the others who are with you will cross the bridge in perfect safety."

Cressingham interceded however, complaining that a large amount of money had already been spent to subdue the revolution. A swift victory was required, and the English army was to cross the river immediately.

When slightly more than half of the English army had reached the other side, Wallace and Moray activated their trap. The Scottish rebels charged down the causeway with their long spears, while their comrades crossed the river to block the bridge's north end. With the archers on the Scots' side of the river, the English could not rely on their deadly range. Cressingham was killed alongside five thousand English soldiers, elevating the Battle of Stirling to Scotland's most significant victory against the English army since the Dark Ages. With Andrew Moray fatally wounded, Wallace did not have to share the credit for the momentous victory.

Wallace was hailed as the leader and savior of Scotland and embraced by the commoners (his popularity amongst the Scottish nobles was not as forthcoming). After his success at Stirling, Wallace forced the English army at Dundee to surrender. He reclaimed control of Cupar Castle, but was unable to force the English out of Edinburg Castle, Dunbar Castle, Berwick Castle, and Roxburgh Castle. With the exception of such strongholds, he managed to force a large portion of the English army out of Scotland. He also defeated Earl Patrick, an important Scottish magnate that refused to switch allegiances (he also insulted Wallace for his lowly origins).

Once Earl Patrick had been defeated, Wallace was able to turn the tables on Berwick, a previously Scottish settlement which had defected following a defeat the previous year. Wallace led his troops into the settlement, turning the small village into a scene of brutal carnage. Soon after Berwick, Wallace led his men south into Northumberland and Cumbria. The population of Northumbria had recently witnessed the previously undefeated English army fleeing southward and quickly followed suit, evacuating the area with all available food and cattle, leaving nothing for the Scots to scavenge.

By the time Wallace's army had reached Cumbria, however, they demonstrated that they had learned from previous mistakes. They moved far more carefully, claiming all the food and supplies available in the area before returning to Northumberland. This left them strong and well-equipped.

Wallace had no intention of attacking the fortresses which housed the remaining English Garrisons in Scotland, however he made an exception at Carlisle. Carlisle Castle was located at a strategic point on the western entry of Scotland, one which could not be left in English hands if the Scots were to secure control of Scotland. Wallace sent a large force to surround the Castle, yet had no plans to assault it. The rest of his army was sent to Newcastle to burn the town of Ryton to the ground after its inhabitants taunted the Scots from across the Tyne, its citizens having never thought that the army would wade across the river to retaliate!

Over the course of weeks, Wallace rampaged through northern England, burning over seven hundred English villages. Wallace's forces killed thousands of people in their rage, and those who were left had no will to resist the Scottish invaders. Thus, the army had free reign to pillage hundreds of villages and towns, taking most of their food and possessions.

The Scottish dominance in northern England came to an end not long before Christmas, with the English leading a counterattack under Sir Robert De Clifford. Several thousand English foot soldiers killed over three hundred Scotsmen at Annandale. By the time the English advance halted at Christmas, they had ten villages and towns. They had reclaimed the town of Annan and destroyed the church at Gisburn. Innocents on both sides of the Scottish border would suffer immeasurably in this time, as the Scotsmen withdrew to the north.

Wallace reached the height of his powers during late 1297 and early 1298, when he was knighted as the Guardian of Scotland. This honor gave him the power to act on behalf of the entire Scottish realm – with the backing and consent of the magnates. There were undoubtedly many magnates who were opposed to the idea of a young man without prestigious origins becoming their leader, but Wallace had already won the people's hearts and had the backing of a surprisingly successful army. The Scottish knights, earls, and barons had also discredited themselves with their notoriously shaky allegiances.

Unfortunately for Wallace, the Scottish earls were ultimately unable to provide him with their undivided support. Wallace attempted to unite the disorganized and divided kingdom, but many of Scottish nobles could not put aside their envy and wounded pride to accept that they had been outranked by a commoner – even for the greater good. They were nevertheless loyal enough to Wallace to remain absent from a parliament session that Edward called for on 14 January 1298. This absence marked them as public enemies of England, and served as a sign for how Edward's control over Scotland had been diminished.

Only death would put an end to Edward's ambitions to conquer Scotland. (He would come to be known as "Scottorum malleus" – the Hammer of the Scots - after his death).[xxxix] Undeterred by the English earls' indignant stance towards the financial costs of all of his foreign invasions, he began raising money to mount a decisive counter-attack against Wallace. He mobilized the Welsh troops and assembled an army of fourteen thousand horsemen and one hundred thousand foot soldiers; the largest army to be amassed against the Scots thus far.

John de Warenne, anxious to redeem himself after the battle of Stirling Bridge, led the massive English force on to Roxburgh, securing a quick triumph. The sheer size of the army allowed for several other swift victories, with Berwick surrendering. It was only at Kelso that the presence of Wallace's own cavalry halted further progress into the hills. At Berwick, Warenne received communication from Edward that he was returning from France to take supreme command over the Scottish invasion. Warenne was instructed to stay put at Berwick until Edward arrived.

To his credit, Wallace made extensive preparations to prepare for his ultimate confrontation with England's military might. He organized Scotland into military districts and began conscripting all able-bodied Scottish males that were older than sixteen. He established a merit-based chain of command, doing away with the feudal hierarchies that privileged members of the landowning classes in the military. He placed ambitious and able common men in the clergy, law enforcement, and the administrative workforce. While the Scotsmen were generally eager to join the growing army of its legendary leader, Wallace still left prudent reminders as to the consequences awaiting those who ignored his conscription regulations. He had gallows erected in every town, village, and burgh.

Wallace also turned to the clergy in his mission for reform, appointing William de Lamberton, an earlier supporter of Wallace, as head of St. Andrews. With Lamberton in a position of power, Wallace removed all English priests from the clergy, purging the ranks of those men that had been placed there by Edward. Some of the English priests and nuns that were removed were killed in the process.

Two towns in the Lothians and Berwickshire were destroyed to prevent the English access to food and supplies when they arrived.

Wallace's scorched earth strategy proved to be effective in thwarting Edward's large army (approximately 87,500 men), whose morale became crippled by hunger when English supply ships were compromised by itinerant weather and Scottish pirates.

Wallace also devised a new military formation; one designed specifically to combat the English heavy cavalry which was so effective against the lightly armored Scottish footmen. The tactic was named the schiltron. Foot soldiers would utilize twelve-foot long spears to create a hedgehog-like defensive formation, with spear points poised in all directions. With the foot soldiers also carrying shields, the Scottish infantry was in a better position to survive the English archers as well as the charge of the heavily armored English Knights.

Edward returned to England and began laying down his plans to invade the north, testing the strength of the Scottish defenses as well as the people's will to resist. Edward began moving up large quantities of supplies to Carlisle, with more supplies being amassed in England to be shipped to Berwick and Edinburgh once they were reclaimed. All this was in preparation of the main invasion which took place on 25 June 1298.

Edward arrived at Roxburgh on the 24 June to an army that was comprised of four thousand light horsemen, three thousand heavy cavalry, and eighty thousand foot soldiers. Of the eighty thousand foot soldiers, a majority of them were troops hired from Ireland and Wales. The English marched from Roxburgh to eventually engage Wallace's army at the Battle of Falkirk.

Edwards massive army came with massive logistical problems. Despite the supplies that had been prepared prior to the army's departure, feeding the army was still a laborious and difficult task. It was not made easier by Wallace's scorched earth strategy, which left the English nothing to forage while on the move into Scotland. Edward attempted to lift the morale of his troops by distributing two hundred casks of wine from supply ships that had managed to evade

Scottish pirates. However, this simply led to infighting between the English and Welsh troops, further demoralizing the hungry army.

With the army suffering attrition and low morale, Edward ordered his troops to withdraw to Edinburgh to wait for supplies. It was at Edinburgh that Edward was informed of the sighting of the Scottish army, eighteen miles away in the forest of Selkirk. By 9 a.m. that day the English army was marching towards Falkirk, arriving at Linlithgow by nightfall. Scottish cavalry was spotted the next day, and the English army moved towards the fields of Falkirk.

Wallace would have had a longer political and military career if he had out-waited the English army longer. Instead of continuously eluding them in the Scottish countryside and waiting for them to retreat due to fatigue and acute food shortages, Wallace's army engaged Edward's men in an ill-advised direct confrontation at the Battle of Falkirk.

Wallace had the schiltron – his new military formation devised to confront the English cavalry. However, he could not have anticipated the deadly range of the Welshmen and Lancastrians' longbow. This recent military invention was as comparable to medieval warfare as poison gas had been to modern warfare.

Edward initially ordered the Welsh to advance against the Scottish schiltron. However, they refused to be used as guinea pigs, forcing Edward to instead order forth the English Cavalry. As the cavalry advanced, they found that the seemingly sturdy meadows were hiding swampy grounds. Unable to advance, the heavy cavalry was forced to find a way around the bog. The second line of cavalry advanced more warily, heading towards the eastern side of the swamp, awaiting the third advance line led by Edward himself.

Wallace's schiltrons were in a position to cover all four lines of the English cavalry; his footmen were disciplined and well-armed with their spears. The English cavalry was unwilling to directly confront this hedgehog-like formation, and so turned their attention to the Scottish archers.

While the cavalry made quick work of the Scottish archers, Edward ordered the advance of the infantry, including the Lancastrian bowmen, who let fly their arrows at incredible range. The Scotsmen simply had no defense against the ceaseless rain of arrows that showered down from the sky – accompanied by the flurry of stones and rocks hurled by the English infantry. As the once-impregnable schiltrons floundered under the endless hail of arrows and projectiles, Wallace's men abandoned their ranks to retreat. The English knights then rode them down, culling the men in close combat – where their twelve-foot spears were practically useless.

Wallace managed to escape with a few surviving members of his army. His infantry (which was once ten thousand men strong) had been massacred, but the Scottish cavalry had wisely decided to retreat and fight the English in more favorable conditions. Wallace's reputation as a military leader had been permanently maimed. He gave up his Guardianship of Scotland soon afterwards, and returned to life as an outlaw. During his retreat from the English army, he ordered for the towns of Stirling and Perth to be destroyed. When the supply ships Edward was expecting from Ireland and west England failed to arrive, the English army suffered from a fifteen-day famine. Edward was thus forced to abandon his plans to completely eradicate what remained of Scotland's resistance forces.

For the next seven years, Edward ordered his troops to attack Scotland annually. Wallace's life was largely anti-climactic during this time. He harassed the English whenever he could with his tightly-knit band of outlaws, while also occasionally traveling abroad to win the support of King Phillip of France, Eric II of Norway, and the Pope. Wallace's diplomatic efforts were ultimately unsuccessful. By 1304, the Scottish nobility surrendered and agreed to sign an agreement with Edward. After he accepted the submission of the Scottish nobility, Edward himself led an attack on Stirling Castle – the last stronghold that defied English rule.

Edward ordered the castle be blockaded, preventing supplies from reaching the defenders. Massive siege engines were shipped in from

Edinburgh, and Stirling Castle's walls would be tested by the greatest artillery the English possessed at the time. On April 22, Edward took control of the siege operations at Stirling. The English siege arsenal was varied. For example, there were thirteen trebuchets each capable of hurling a stone weighing three hundred pounds over a thousand yards. There were other specialized machines used for pulling their own galleries and parapets, rams for tackling the gates, and even a mobile tower that was capable of lifting a cage of twenty men over the walls of the castle.

The defenders did not succumb without a fight, unleashing boiling oil and molten lead on the attackers. However, the lack of supplies was taking a toll. On 20 July 1304, the Scottish rebels finally succumbed to Edward's demand for an absolute and unconditional surrender. The leader of the rebels of Stirling, Sir William Oliphant, was imprisoned in the tower of London, leaving Wallace now as the lone figure in opposition to the English. With a bounty of three hundred marks on Wallace's head and Edward's determination to capture him, Wallace had no chance of victory and little chance of survival.

Edward was merciful to the Scottish magnates who opposed him, only offering public humiliation, banishment for a few years, or exile; he seemed only to harbor a hatred for Wallace. Edward forced Scottish leaders to hunt Wallace down in return for more lenient punishments for their insurrection. Despite the offer, none of these men took any serious action towards hunting down the legendary Scot.

Wallace was ultimately betrayed by his own servant, Jack Short, and Sir John Menteith, a trusted Scottish baron who had been tempted by Edward's promise of wealth and land titles. Edward specifically selected John Menteith to hunt down Wallace as the man knew him personally, Wallace being the godfather to Menteith's two sons.

In Blind Harry's epic poem, Menteith was apparently reluctant to execute his mission. It was only after he was written to personally by

Edward that he arranged for his nephew to join Wallace's guerrilla band, to keep track of Wallace's movements. Wallace had ridden out of Robroyston, hoping to meet with Robert Bruce, the man he believed could restore Scottish independence whereas he could not. Menteith's nephew quickly informed him of the plan, and with sixty of his most loyal men he rode out to intercept Wallace's much larger force.

No fight was to occur between the two forces as Menteith waited for nightfall before coming upon Wallace's camp. Wallace's right-hand man was killed before Wallace himself was dragged from the bed he shared with his mistress. Hopelessly outnumbered, Wallace still attempted to fight off Menteith's men with his bare hands. Blind Harry mentions that Wallace was deceived, Menteith had stated that the area was surrounded by a much larger force than the one he had actually brought along. Naively, Wallace agreed to be bound hand and foot and escorted to Dumbarton Castle under the protection of Menteith.

For this Menteith was rewarded handsomely. Edward's note had requested that Menteith capture Wallace alive in order to allow for a humiliating death that would destroy the legend's reputation and further demoralize the defeated Scots.

After being captured, he was put through a show trial in Westminster and quickly found guilty of sedition, homicide, robbery, arson, and other crimes.

The trial was important for impressing upon both the English and Scottish the depravity to which Wallace had stooped in his ungodly insurrection against the English Crown. English propaganda had painted a picture of the gigantic young man as "an ogre of unspeakable depravity who skinned his prisoners alive, burned babies, and forced nuns to dance naked for him." Wallace's English reputation also extended to a torturer of priests, rapist of nuns, and murderer of women and children by fire and sword.

No opportunity for defense was given to Wallace, and he was given no lawyer nor any opportunity to speak against the charges laid against him. The murder of the Sheriff of Lanark by Wallace was singled out as the event catalyst which sparked the Scottish insurrection against the "rightful" lord of Scotland, Edward. Wallace did, however, make sure to loudly declare to all that could hear that he could not be guilty of treason, having never pledged allegiance to Edward.

Wallace was executed at Westminster on the 23 August 1305 as a large English crowd cheered on. Wallace's death was seen as fairly standard procedure for those found guilty of treason during this period.[xl] Wallace was stripped naked before being led to the execution grounds. Drawn by horses, the naked Scot was led from the Palace of Westminster to the Tower of London and then through the city to the Elms. Garbage and excrement were thrown at him by jeering English crowds.

Once Wallace reached the Elms he was taken from the cart to the gallows. There he was hung but taken down before his neck could break. His genitals were removed and he was disemboweled, his intestines pulled out to be burned. His internal organs followed as the executioner removed liver and lungs. His final death came at the removal of his heart from his body. English mobs cheered as his head was cut off with a cleaver. All of this was intended to humiliate and degrade the Scottish hero. His body was then quartered; cut into four pieces.

His head was hung up on the London Bridge, while the four quarters were sent to Newcastle-upon-Tyne, Berwick, Stirling, and St. Johnson "as a warning and a deterrent to all that pass by and behold them." Edward intended for Wallace's fate to be a traumatic warning to anyone in Scotland who dared to resist his rule, but Wallace would prove to be more powerful in death than he had been in life. He lived on as a folk hero and a martyr of the highest order – an immortal symbol of the lengths and depths that Scotland was willing to go to free itself from the cursed yoke of English oppression.

Chapter 5 – Power Struggles

Wallace's legendary patriotic zeal – during and after his lifetime - may have inspired many Scottish elites to defect from Edward and believe in their ability to resist English rule, but he was never able to unite them. After Wallace's fall from grace, the Scottish nobility was still divided along the fault lines that had first appeared during Scotland's succession crisis.

After Wallace's career as the Guardian of Scotland ended, a fragile truce was established between two rival nobles: John Comyn and Robert the Bruce. Comyn was a nephew of John Balliol, the exiled King of Scotland. The Comyns were a powerful northern noble family with significant military resources, and were personally invested in arranging for the exiled King John to return to Scotland. Robert the Bruce shared the same name as his grandfather – who had competed with John Balliol for the Scottish throne in 1290 – and harbored similar royal ambitions.

By May of 1300, Bruce was unable to put up the pretense of supporting Balliol's return and resigned from the position of joint Guardian. By 1304, however, John Balliol had resigned himself to the fact that he would never be able to return to his throne. Scotland's diplomatic maneuvers had come to naught. The Pope needed Edward's military support for his latest crusade against Islam. After the death of his first wife Eleanor, Edward shrewdly arranged for his marriage to Marguerite – King Philip's seventeen-year-old sister – to broker a treaty of peace with France. King Philip and Pope Boniface ended up in an open war against each other, resulting in the Pope's death. As the de facto leader of the Scottish nobility, Comyn headed the peace negotiations with Edward on 9 February 1304. This capitulation was a death sentence for all hopes that Balliol would be restored to the Scottish throne. Bruce's own father also died in 1304 – leaving him as the sole claimant to the throne.

Two years and one day later, the single most decisive political murder in Scottish history occurred. John Comyn met Robert Bruce at the Greyfriars monastery in Dumfries, presumably on peaceful terms now that Edward's rule over Scotland had been formally accepted by all the nobles. It is also unclear if it was Robert Bruce or his followers which dealt the coup de grâce, but Comyn was left dead by a fatal knife wound on the church altar.

Bruce's intentions for killing Comyn remain murky, as does his legacy as *the* freedom fighter that finally secured Scotland's independence. When compared to Wallace's pure, unambiguous patriotism, Bruce certainly appeared to be far more opportunistic, self-serving, and calculative. (One should remember, however, that it was exceedingly common for Scottish nobles of the time to switch sides in order to pursue power). Bruce and his father had supported Edward I when he invaded Scotland in 1296, with hopes of securing the crown for their lineage after Balliol was displaced. During the tumultuous rebellions against English rule between 1295 and 1304, Bruce alternated between being one of Wallace's leading supporters and a trusted ally to Edward. Bruce had switched sides several times, being a Guardian of Scotland during a period of resistance, and then switching sides back to Edward during the loss of the battle of Falkirk. While Bruce's switching of sides can be considered inconsistent and fickle, his actions were similar to those of all other nobles with lands and estates, whose loyalties were to family and fortune first.

Under encouragement from Bishop Wishart, Bruce had raised the standard of revolt at Irvine in 1297. This meant his absence from the legendary Battle of Stirling Bridge. After his uprising failed and Wallace emerged victorious, Bruce did not join his ranks. Instead he maintained a low profile and waited to see how the English would respond to the unexpected defeat. Bruce had also been absent at the calamitous Battle of Falkirk.

There was thus no evidence from this time – and certainly no prophecy – that would suggest his eventual transformation into a leader of Scotland's war of independence. In any case, it is unlikely that Bruce murdered Comyn for any abstract ideals pertaining to Scottish pride and honor. Bruce ostensibly either (1) assassinated Comyn in cold-blood to pave the way to the throne; or (2) killed him out of rage – their rivalry had certainly incurred political and financial costs on his side – and then improvised a bid for the throne.

Historians are unsure of what transpired during that fateful meeting, but they are clear on the consequences of Comyn's death. Given Bruce's possible motives for killing Comyn, the Pope decided to punish him for committing murder in a holy place. Bruce was excommunicated (i.e. banished from the Catholic Church) for this sacrilege. This was a severe blow to Bruce's royal ambitions, as the Church would have conferred legitimacy and protection to his status as a rightful monarch. Undeterred, he proceeded to claim the throne for himself. Bruce did have the support of Robert Wishart, the Bishop of Glasgow and one of Wallace's key supporters. Wishart convinced Bruce to seize the throne and helped to organize his coronation. On the 25th of March, Bruce hastened to Scone and was crowned as the King of Scotland (the Stone of Scone and Scottish Crown Jewels were absent from the ceremony).

Bruce may have secured the throne with seemingly little effort, but his unexpected position was King was exceedingly difficult. Edward had firm control over the majority of Scotland's important castles and deemed him to be a traitor. Many of the other Scottish nobles had been allied to Comyn and John Balliol and did not attend Bruce's crowning ceremony. With a possible civil war on his hands and Edward's wrath on his head, Bruce's position was exceedingly precarious.

He did not have to wait long to suffer for his audacious royal ambitions. In June 1306, he endured his first defeat against Edward's army at the Battle of Methven. Led by Aymer de Valence, 2nd Earl of Pembroke,[xli] the English force took Bruce's army by surprise and nearly eradicated it completely. Bruce escaped with a few followers towards his homelands in the southwest, leaving his two clerical supporters - William de Lamberton and Robert Wishart – to languish in an English dungeon. (Since they were holy men, they were spared from execution).

Bruce suffered from more personal and military losses even while he was traveling towards his lands. His own men were intercepted by John MacDougall and his men. A Comyn supporter, MacDougall was bent on revenge for John Comyn's murder at Greyfriars. Bruce was lucky to survive the Battle of Dalry in July 1306, which nearly eliminated all of his surviving supporters. Bruce was now practically a fugitive, hounded by the English and his Scottish opponents.

He was then forced to endure traumatic personal losses. His wife, daughter, and two sisters had been traveling with him and his men, but he decided to send them to Kildrummy Castle out of concerns for their safety. They were escorted by his younger brother Neil. In September, the English attacked the castle and forced the Scots to surrender. Neil was hung, drawn and beheaded (like Wallace) – a devastating blow to Bruce (the eldest brother) and his remaining three brothers (Edward, Thomas, and Alexander). The English also captured Bruce's wife, daughter, and two sisters and placed them under house arrest. As hostages, they could be useful pawns in a negotiation with Bruce if he ever rose to power. Mary Bruce and Isabella, the Countess of Buchan, were both imprisoned in cages that were hung from their respective castles (Berwick and Roxburgh) to deter other rebels.

Chapter 6 – Inner Strife

The fall and winter of 1306 was the lowest point in Bruce's career.[xlii] He was forced to flee from the Scottish mainland, and earned the unenviable nickname of King Hob ("King Nobody") during this time. His exact hideout during this trying period remains unknown, but historians speculate that he hid out in a cave on Rathlin Island, which lies between Kintyre and County Antrim in Northern Ireland. While Bruce was absent, the English captured two more of his brothers: Thomas and Alexander. Both were executed. Bruce is purported to have retained his hope and patience from watching a spider persevere in its seemingly futile and foolish attempts to spin a web from one area of the cave's roof to another (alternate versions of the story replace the cave's roof with two roof means). After failing twice, it achieved its objective on its third attempt.

In February 1307, Bruce returned to the Scottish mainland to face his opponents a third time. His primary supporter was Edward, his last surviving brother. Bruce and Edward gathered more supporters from their family lands at Carrick. After his early disasters, Bruce had reached the wise conclusion that he could never defeat the English in a traditional battle. Like Wallace, he stood the best chance by relying on ambushes, surprise attacks, guerrilla tactics, and unconventional military strategies:

"Let Scotland's warcraft be this: footsoldiers, mountains and marshy ground; and let her woods, her bow and spear serve for barricades. Let menace lurk in all her narrow places among her warrior bands, and let her plains so burn with fire that her enemies flee away. Crying out in the night, let her men be on their guard, and her enemies in confusion will flee from hunger's sword. Surely it will be so, as we're guided by Robert, our lord."

- *Scotland's Strategy of Guerrilla Warfare (c.1308)*[xliii]

In April, Bruce secured his first minor victory against the English with the Battle of Glen Trool.[xliv] His strategy of ambushing John Mowbray and his men by charging down the steep hillsides proved to be highly effective. The following month, Bruce redeemed his military reputation by defeating Aymer de Valence at the Battle of Loudoun Hill. This time, Bruce gained the upper hand via the same "bottleneck" circumstances that had tipped the scale in Wallace's favor at the Battle of Stirling Bridge. Valence had the larger army, but his men were hindered by a large bog and the parallel ditches that Bruce's men had dug out.

Valence had been in charge of the main English force in Scotland. This victory undoubtedly boosted the hopes and confidence of Bruce and his supporters. It was more empowering, however, to learn the news of Edward I's death. While traveling with the aims of reconquering Scotland once and for all, he died at Burgh-on-Sands after falling ill near the Scottish border. His son and successor, Edward II, decided to head south to secure his position as the new King of England – instead of confronting Bruce. Edward II gave some of the highest offices in England to his father's most noteworthy opponents – which earned him much antagonism from the barons.

A large portion of the conflict between Edward II and the barons revolved around Piers Gaveston,[xlv] Edward II's former playmate and foster brother. Edward I himself was responsible for introducing his household to Gaveston. He was a few years older than Edward II, and was deemed a positive role model for his military prowess, athleticism, and good manners. By 1303, Gaveston was designated as *socious* (companion) instead of a *scutifer* (esquire). In 1306, both were knighted. However, Edward I banished Gaveston to France later that year for reasons that remain unclear.

Not long after Edward II was crowned, he made Gaveston his chief adviser and made him the Earl of Cornwall (a title that had only be conferred on royalty; Gaveston was the son of a Gascon knight). Gaveston was also granted huge grants of land, and the hand in marriage of Margaret de Clare, Gloucester heiress. The true nature of Edward II and Gaveston's unusually close relationship is difficult to ascertain. Some historians have argued that they had entered into a "brotherhood-in-arms," while others argue that they were actually lovers (some speculate that Edward I had banished Gaveston to make way for his son's marriage to Isabella of France).[xlvi] It is nevertheless clear that Gaveston's "undue" wealth, position, status, and arrogance incited the jealousy and anger of the barons, Edward II's young wife Isabella, and his father-in-law King Philip of France. Chroniclers of the era lamented the king's love for Gaveston, which was described as "excessive," "inordinate," "immoderate," and "beyond measure and reason."[xlvii]

Regardless of the true nature of their relationship, the idea and practice of royal favorites would not have been such a major cause for concern if Edward II had been an effectual leader.[xlviii] He had inherited a costly Scottish conquest, and the English crown was heavily in debt. He was unable to raise an army to combat Robert the Bruce, but nevertheless taxed the English people and forcibly seized crops from them. Edward II was easily distracted, inept at military affairs, thoughtless, and weak. Instead of addressing pressing military and administrative matters, Edward was often hiding away in his chambers with Gaveston. By allowing the barons to become royal enemies instead of royal allies, Edward II sealed his place in history as the worst of England's Plantagenet kings.

In 1311, a baronial committee consisting of 21 members drafted the "Ordinances"[xlix] – a document that called for Gaveston to be permanently banished from England and for Edward II's powers over important appointments and finances to be restricted. It was passed in November that year, but Gaveston boldly defied it by returning to England in January the following year. Edward II publicly restored him, which enraged the barons. Thomas of Lancaster, Edward's cousin and the most powerful baron in landed terms, sentenced Gaveston to death after he was captured by baronial forces in 1312.

Instead of restoring the English government, however, Gaveston's death only lead to more civil strife. The English were divided between Lancaster supporters and those who felt that the murder was a breach of justice (even if they were happy to see Gaveston eliminated). Two other problematic figures which exerted a more negative influence than Gaverston ever did eventually appeared at Edward II's side as his new favorites: Hugh Despenser the Elder and his son, Hugh Despenser the Younger.[1]

Edward II's ineffectual leadership and drawn out, ultimately doomed campaign against the powerful English barons certainly worked in Bruce's favor, as it gave him more time to solidify his own position. Unlike his English counterpart, he would prove successful in bending the Scottish noble to his will. His first objective was to defeat John Comyn's supporters. As the English courts were embroiled in inner strife in the winter between 1307and 1308, Bruce marched northeast towards the northern Comyn lands. He defeated the Earl of Ross and captured the castles in the Great Glen. He gained control of Inverlochy, Urquhart, and Inverness.

In 1308, Bruce journeyed eastwards towards the Comyn castles of Banff, Balvenie and Duffus in Buchan. He attacked the Black Isle despite being perilously ill. He successfully defeated John Comyn, the 3rd Earl of Buchan (the cousin of John III Comyn, which Bruce murdered at Greyfriars and Bruce's primary opponent), at the Battle of Inverurie in May. Bruce's men also defeated the English garrison at Aberdeen. To ensure that the Comyn family was thoroughly defeated, he ordered the Harrying of Buchan in 1308. Buchan was the agricultural hub of northern Scotland and a Comyn stronghold (support for the family was strong even after Comyn was defeated).

Bruce had large swaths of farmland burned, livestock slain, and Comyn supporters murdered. The Comyn castles in Moray, Aberdeen, and Buchan were ruined.

During the autumn of 1308, Bruce turned his sights on the MacDougall clan in Argyll, longtime allies of the Comyns in the southwest. After claiming Dunstaffnage Castle at the Battle of Pass of Brander, Bruce had successfully wiped out the MacDougall army and defeated the Comyn's final major stronghold. After controlling northern and southwestern Scotland for a century and a half, the Comyn family was obliterated. Bruce assumed control of the entirety of northern Scotland by March of 1309.[li]

Emboldened by his domestic victories, he called for his first parliament at St. Andrews that month. His position as the King of Scotland was supported by the remaining nobles and a letter from Philip of France. A year later, the Scottish bishops recognized his claim to the throne (despite his excommunication from the Catholic Church) in the Declaration of the Clergy - a document which absolved him of the sins of his past. Despite the Pope's interdict (which suspended all Church activities in Scotland following Bruce's excommunication), the Scottish bishops remained unflinching Bruce supporters. He was, after all, their only hope for the Scottish Church's separate existence and legitimacy (Bruce's defeat would mean endless interferences from the English Church).[lii]

By 1310, Bruce no longer had to contend with opponents on his home soil. He turned his gaze southward, to the Lowlands that lay southwards of the River Tay – Scottish territory that was still under English control.

Chapter 7 – The Battle of Bannockburn

After failing to negotiate a truce with Edward II, Bruce began to forcefully recapture the Scottish castles and important outposts occupied by the English in the Lowlands. Linlithgow was reclaimed in 1310, Dumbarton in 1311, and Perth was won by Bruce himself in January 1312.[liii] Despite being stepped in the code of honor and military tactics of a feudal knight, Bruce provided to be as effective (or more) of a guerrilla fighter as Wallace. Bruce even extended his military excursions into northern England, capturing Castle Rushen in Castletown and occupying the entire Isle of Man – an island of significant strategic importance to the English.

As Bruce continued to harass English troops and the northern English towns, his brother Edward Bruce surrounded Stirling Castle. By this time, it was the final key stronghold that still remained under English control. Its governor, Philip de Mowbray, held off the Scottish attackers, but agreed to surrender if reinforcements from Edward II did not arrive by the midsummer of 1314. Edward II received the news by May and hastened towards the key fortification from Berwick. His force – which consisted of approximately 3,000 cavalry and 13,000 infantry (including a contingent of Welsh archers) - reached the southward part of Stirling by the following month. This was the largest English army to have ever invaded Scotland. (Edward II had actually summoned 25,000 infantry from England, Ireland and Wales, but only half of them reported for duty).

Robert Bruce's force had already arrived, ready to compensate for their much smaller numbers (7,000 infantry and a few hundred cavalry). Most of Bruce's footmen were armed with pikes,[liv] a long spear that consisted of a heavy wooden shaft (between 3 – 6 meters in length) and a leaf-shaped steel point. They were led by the King, his brother Edward, and his nephew Sir Thomas Randolph (the Earl of Moray).[iv] Each leader was in command of a single division of schiltrons. Eight years of victorious guerrilla warfare against the English and their Scottish opponents had shaped Bruce's men into an experienced and tough fighting force.

Bruce assembled his men at the New Park: a royal hunting preserve that lay between 1-2 miles (1.6 – 3.2 km) south of Stirling. His strategy was to use the tree formations there to funnel the English army directly towards his heavily armed footmen and recently excavated anti-cavalry ditches. When the English army arrived on June 23rd, his traps were ready. The road to Stirling was blocked by the Scottish army, prompting the English to meet the Scots on disadvantageous terrain.

On the 23rd June, Edward II sent out two different scouting parties to survey the area before his main force advanced further. The party led by the Earl of Hereford stumbled upon Bruce himself, as he was inspecting the strength and numbers of the English troops. An English knight named Henry de Bohun charged directly towards Bruce. (If he successfully killed or captured Bruce, he would receive a lifetime of praise as a war hero). After quickly sidestepping Bohun's lance, Bruce killed him with a single blow of his battle axes (to the back of the head). Hereford was then forced to retreat back towards the English camp by Bruce's supporters. Meanwhile, the Earl of Moray and his schiltron fought back the rest of the advancing English forces. Two of Edward II's experienced commanders, Sir Henry Beaumont and Sir Robert Clifford, were forced to retreat after a violent confrontation. Without the Welsh archers, the English knights were ill-equipped to confront the Scots' formidable thicket of spears. Their swords and maces were useless against the advancing schiltrons, which moved forward slowly and eventually forced them to take flight. (This offensive use of the schiltrons was a new tactic; Wallace had only used them as a form of static defense).

The Scots thus emerged the victors on the first day of the Battle of Bannockburn. Edward II decided to relocate his army closer to the banks of the Bannock-burn that evening (out of fears that Bruce would attack them in the night). This was an inevitably unhelpful decision, as his men suffered from poor sleep on the wet and marshy grounds.

The next morning, the Scottish army assumed their planned battle formation against a sleep-deprived and disorganized English force. The English nevertheless hoped to restage Wallace's defeat at the Battle of Falkirk. In a full-scale direct confrontation, Welsh longbowmen would be able to take on the Scottish schiltrons in a clean sweep. To Edward II's delight, Bruce decided to risk everything and face the English in an open battle. This was no reckless decision. At this critical point in time, a Scottish noble in the English army had switched sides and brought crucial intelligence to Bruce. Sir Alexander Seton reported that the English were suffering from low morale. He also revealed their confined position.

Even if the circumstances were fortuitous, the Scottish army was still taking on a grave risk. To be on the safe side, Bruce had planned for a strategic retreat if the outcome of the battle was not in his favor. The judgment of God was deemed to be a critical factor in such medieval battles (this is why the Scottish's clergy's decision to pardon Bruce's transgressions was so important). In the heart of one of the Scots' schiltrons, Abbot Bernard of Arbroath held tightly to an aged talisman: the Breccbennach (it contained the relics of St. Columba). Bruce roused his men with an inspiring speech that referenced St. Andrew, John the Baptist and Thomas Beckett.

Before the met the English the battle, the Scots held mass on the battlefield. Abbot Maurice of Inchafrrey led the Scots in religious worship, as they all knelt in prayer. Upon witnessing this, Edward II purportedly stated "Yon folk are kneeling to ask mercy." Sir Ingram de Umfraville, a supporter for Balliol who was fighting for the English, translated the essence of the prayer to him: "They ask for mercy, but not from you. They ask God for mercy for their sins. I'll tell you something for a fact, that yon men will win all or die. None will flee for fear of death." Edward II was not intimidated. "So be it," he responded.[lvi]

Bruce had chosen his battleground wisely: the boggy ground made it difficult for the English cavalry to advance or to launch effective counterattacks. After a brief archery duel, the Scottish schiltrons began advancing rapidly to negate the Welsh longbowmen's deadly advantage in long-range combat. The three formidable formations closed in on the English. Edward Bruce's schiltron attacked the English vanguard, killing Sir Robert Clifford and the Earl of Glouchester. Meanwhile, Randolph's schiltron advanced towards the left flank of the English army. The English archers occasionally found an effective position to open fire on the Scots, but the Scottish cavalry soon charged at them and forced them to retreat from the field. Some of them were even counter-effective; their arrows landed onto the backs of the English army. As the English retreated slowly, the ditches that Bruce's men had dug turned into traps for many English knights. Once they fell in, the English knights and their horses were unable to escape.

A life-or-death clash between English swords and Scottish spears took place in the heart of the field. The ultimate outcome depended on the outcome of this intense hand-to-hand combat. Bruce and his schiltron advanced into this crucial melee, bringing the Gaelic warriors from the Highlands and Islands into the fray. Their presence slowly and surely tipped the scales. As the English began to fall back, the Scots yelled "On them! On them! They fail!"

As the English were driven back by a final and forceful push from the Scottish soldiers and dissolved into a disorganized mess, Edward II was reluctantly escorted away. As the royal standard fled from the battlefield, the English soldiers began to panic. The Scottish schiltrons advanced on the disarrayed English army, slaughtering the English as they attempted to escape. Hundreds of English men and horses drowned in the burn as they made a desperate bid to escape from the merciless Scots.

Edward II himself made a narrow escape to Dunbar, where he made a safe exit to England via ship. Sir James "the Black" Douglas had pursued Edward II and his royal guard of 500 knights all the way to Dunbar. If he had been captured, this would have forced the English to instantly grant Bruce all of his demands. Edward II was lucky, but many of his men were doomed. By the time the battle of ended, thousands of footmen lay dead. A hundred knights and one earl had fallen. The Earl of Pembroke and his Welsh infantry retreated successful to Carlisle, but the Earl of Hereford and several other knights were pursued and captured as they fled southwards. (The Scots reported – perhaps inaccurately – that they had only lost two knights and a few hundred infantrymen).

Without Edward II's capture or death, the English could still continue their war against Bruce. The Scots had nevertheless emerged with *the* major victory against the English during the Middle Ages. Bruce and his commanders had also earned a place in military history. The Battle of Bannockburn[lvii] and the Battle of the Golden Spurs[lviii] in 1302 was eventually credited with the introduction of a new form of European warfare, where the infantry were the critical players on the battlefield (instead of the cavalry). With Stirling Castle under his control, Bruce had now acquired complete military control of Scotland. He could now direct his attention towards northern England. (Wallace had been in a similarly enviable position after the Battle at Stirling Bridge).

Bruce also had more personal victories to look forward to. Now that he had consolidated his kingship, Balliol's stalwart supporters were finally motivated to switch allegiances. To obtain the freedom of the English noblemen that had been captured, Edward II was forced to release a few highly significant political prisoners: Bruce's wife Elizabeth de Burgh, his daughter Marjorie, and the Bishop of Wishart. Meanwhile, the Scottish soldiers claimed all the wealth, weapons and provisions that the English had been forced to leave behind.

Chapter 8 – A Worthy King

Bruce's military accomplishments may have rivaled – and even eclipsed – Wallace's after the Battle of Bannockburn, but he still had much insecurity about his reputation. Bruce intended to not only claim the throne of Scotland through sheer military prowess, but also in symbolic terms. His sacrilegious murder of John Comyn needed to be presented as the rightful slaughter of a despicable traitor. He also wanted to advance the case that it was the Bruces, and not John Balliol, who were the rightful heir of the Scottish throne. Any interpretation of his actions as those of an ambitious opportunist needed to be subdued.

There was no question of Bruce's ability to defend Scotland against further English invasions after the Battle of Bannockburn. Between 1315 and 1320, Bruce defeated all the attempts that Edward II could muster. Each invasion ended in a humiliating defeat and a hefty increase to the amount of English funds channeled towards the idea of a Scottish conquest. Between 1315 and 1318, Bruce led his commanders to successfully raid the towns and villages of northern England every year.

Bruce's attempts to attack England from a second front in Ireland in 1315 ultimately proved to be far less successful. His intentions were to force the English to divide their military resources between Ireland and Scotland. Bruce attempted to justify his invasion of Ireland – which was led by his brother Edward – as a righteous endeavor that would free the Irish from English rule. His propaganda campaign for the Irish Wars involved a shared vision of a pan-Gaelic alliance and an emphasis of Scotland and Ireland's shared national ancestry.

Modern historians have pithily described Bruce's campaign for Ireland as "Scotland's Vietnam." After Edward Bruce staged a 300-ship invasion of Ulster, he was crowned as the High King of Ireland in 1316. Historians have suggested that Bruce may have wanted his ambitious brother in this position so that he would not usurp his position. There is also the strategic power of gaining control of the seaboard route to Carlisle.

Some Irish leaders were supportive of this diplomatic logic and ready to reunite with Scotland against their common foe. On the other hand, many Irish people saw little difference between the English and Scottish invasion. The Irish campaign was initially successful. By 1316, Edward Bruce was in a position to gain control of Dublin. Instead, he ordered his troops towards Limerick, where they faced acute problems in receiving their supplies. Edward Bruce was ultimately killed during an ill-conceived assault on antagonistic Irish nobles at the Battle of Faughart in October 1318.[lix]

His body was reportedly hacked into four pieces and dispersed to all four corners of Ireland as a warning to the Scots. His head was preserved in salt in a casket and shipped to his brother. Bruce was forced to retire his lofty vision of a "Pan-Gaelic Greater Scotia" and blamed the failure of his endeavors in Ireland on his brother.

In 1318, Bruce reached a high point in his efforts to force Edward II to accept Scotland's independence by re-capturing Berwick. After Bannockburn, the English leaders lacked the unity needed to successfully quell Scotland's thirst for freedom. When Edward II returned to his court, he was forced into a subservient position by his cousin Thomas of Lancaster. Lancaster capitalized on Edward II's military failures to turn himself into the most powerful man in England by 1315. In the end, however, he was not the competent leader that the English desperately needed during this trying period.

Within three years, a group of moderate barons led by Aymer de Valence had to serve as arbitrators between Edward II and Lancaster. Once again, the costly infighting could be traced to Edward II's royal favorite(s). Hugh le Despenser and his son had ingratiated themselves into the king's affections. History repeated itself in more ways than one when Lancaster banished both Despensers (after Edward ill-advisedly supported the Despenser son's ambitions to acquire land titles in Wales).

Given these conditions, it is not surprising that Edward II was unable to reclaim Berwick when he besieged it in 1319. Led by Thomas Randolph[lx] and James Douglas,[lxi] the Scottish army was launching disastrous raids on Yorkshire at the same time. This forced him to retreat. In time, however, Edward II did manage to triumph over his baronial nemesis. Lancaster was defeated and captured at Boroughbridge, Yorkshire, in March 1322 and was summarily executed.

In the end, Bruce arrived at the conclusion that he would not be able to secure Scotland's independence on the battlefield. The formidable guerrilla leader turned towards diplomacy instead by reversing his excommunication from the Roman Catholic Church. With the help of Scotland's clergy, he wrote and sent a letter to Pope John XXII in 1320.[lxii] The Declaration of Arbroath was a historic document that (1) outlined the reasons for why Scotland should remain an independent kingdom; (2) made attempts to rationalize Bruce's previous actions, and; (3) demonstrated that Bruce had unanimous support from the Scottish nobility. Its mission statement is encapsulated in these bold statements: "Never will we on any conditions be subjected to the lordship of the English. It is in truth not for glory, nor riches, nor honours that we are fighting, but for freedom—for that alone, which no honest man gives up save with life itself." There were actually two more letters that were sent to the Pope from Scotland (all with the same intention of securing Scotland's independence). One was sent by the clergy, and one more from the nobles. The letter sent by the nobles was preserved; the other two were lost to time.

Pope John XXII eventually lifted Bruce's excommunication in October 1328. It was ultimately Edward's hopelessly incompetent leadership, however, that finally allowed Bruce to end the First Scottish War of Independence. By 1325, Edward II's favoritism for the Despensers had alienated another powerful figure in his court: his wife Isabella, queen of England. Like Gaveston, the Despensers had earned the wrath of the barons for quickly becoming inseparable from Edward II and accumulating enormous wealth in the process. Like Gaveston, their insatiable greed was compounded by intolerance and arrogance.

Like many barons, Isabella was discontent with how her husband was treating the English nobility. She herself was disenchanted by how her own English estates had been confiscated by the Despensers. Isabella had attempted to broker peace between her husband and the barons before and after Gaveston's murder in 1312; the Despensers were the final straw. In 1325, Isabella sailed home to France on a diplomatic mission. She successfully intervened in a dispute between her brother, Charles IV of France,[lxiii] and Edward II over the latter's land possessions in France (Guyenne, Ponthieu, and Gascony). The lands were secured for England, provided that Edward paid homage to Charles.

While to Paris, Isabella became the mistress of Roger Mortimer and announced that she would not return to England until the Despensers were removed from court.[lxiv] Mortimer was an English baron who had been exiled for his opposition to the Despensers. In September the following year, Isabella and Mortimer invaded England, ordered for the Despensers to be executed, and deposed Edward. Isabella crowned their son Edward III[lxv] in his place in the first month of 1327. Meanwhile, Edward II was imprisoned until his (possibly violent) death in September that year. (There has nevertheless been recent historical evidence to suggest that his death in 1327 was staged – and that he possibly survived until 1330).

As a young boy, Edward III was in a highly precarious position as the new King of England. Bruce took full advantage of the newly crowned king's vulnerable position by commanding his troops to invade England. Pressured by the unwanted prospect of fighting off the Scottish army and the possibility of a civil war with the rebellious English nobles, Isabella and Mortimer offered Bruce a truce. In 1328, they signed the hard-won Treaty of Edinburgh-Northampton.[lxvi] After years of fighting, Bruce had achieved everything he had dreamed of. The truce dictated that (1) Edward III renounced all claims to overlordship over the kingdom of Scotland; (2) peace between England and Scotland would be brokered by an arranged marriage between Bruce's son David and Edward III's sister Joan, and; (3) England officially recognized Scotland's independence and Bruce's rightful position as the King of Scots.

Chapter 9 – Where Your Heart Is

Bruce's son David was only four years old when he was betrothed to Joan. His birth in 1324 had been crucial for Scotland's peace and prosperity. (If Bruce had died without an heir, another costly battle for succession would have been disastrous). By the time Bruce achieved Scotland's independence, he was old and in poor health. Apart from all of his exertions on the battlefield, he had been suffering from an undiagnosed disease – most probably leprosy – for a long time. A year after he signed the Treaty of Edinburgh-Northampton with Isabella and Mortimer, Robert Bruce died at Cardross, Dumbartonshire.

The Scotland he left behind was in a fairly stable state, earning Bruce the moniker "Good King Robert." In 1314, his parliament had decreed that all Scottish nobles who were still allied to England had to forfeit their lands. The forfeited lands were then re-granted to Bruce's supporters through several charters. This allowed some of Bruce's key supporters such as Sir James Douglas, who was knighted for his contributions to the Battle of Bannockburn, to rise to prominence. Douglas was rewarded with large swaths of land in the Selkirk and Roxburgh counties, which would cement the Douglas family's power in the region for years. Bruce had also successfully resurrected the Scottish administration, which had been mostly dysfunctional since 1296. When he died, the system of exchequer audits was functioning once again.

Bruce's dying wish was also fulfilled. His body was buried at Dunfermline Abbey, the traditional final resting place for Scottish kings. On his deathbed, Bruce had instructed his knights to take his heart on a crusade (he had made a vow to participate in a crusade, which remained unfulfilled due to his poor health). Sir James Douglas and his knights obeyed his orders and took it on a crusade in Spain. Douglas was killed during a battle with the Moors, but Bruce's heart was recovered and brought back to Scotland to be buried in Bruce's location of choice: Melrose Abbey. Like Wallace, Bruce's legendary exploits would live on to touch the hearts and souls of new generations of Scottish people through the form of an epic poem. John Barbour[lxvii] would immortalize his contributions in the 14th-century poem *The Bruce* – the first major work of Scottish literature. Barbour strived for historical accuracy in his art, and went so far as to interview the men who had fought at the Battle of Bannockburn to capture the realities of Bruce's military victory.

In 1921, archeologists discovered a cone-shaped casket that contained a heart while excavating Melrose Abbey.[lxviii] There is no definitive evidence that this particular casket belonged to Bruce, however, since heart burial was a common practice among Scottish royals and aristocrats. The casket and the mummified heart were placed in a lead container and reburied – and then uncovered by another group of archeologists 75 years later.

After being held in Edinburgh for safekeeping for two years, it was reburied in Melrose Abbey (a marker stone commemorates the exact spot). Donald Dewar, Secretary of State for Scotland, observed that the uncertainty of the heart's origins only added to the romance: "There is a strong and proper presumption that this is the heart. But in a sense it does not matter. The casket and the heart are symbols of the man." The simple Scottish sandstone marker over Bruce's final resting place bears a heart, a saltire, and an inscription from *The Bruce*: "A noble hart may have nane ease. Gif freedom failye" (A noble heart cannot be at peace if freedom is lacking).

Chapter 10 – The Son of the Bruce & the Second War for Independence

After the Treaty of Edinburgh-Northampton in 1328, Scotland began the 1330s in a fairly good position. Almost three decades of civil war and war with England had severely sapped the country's resources and morale. However, Robert de Bruce had, for the time being, secured a peaceful end to the English coveting of Scotland. Bruce's death on the 7th of June 1329 left behind a four-year-old son; David II.

David II was crowned king of Scotland on 24 November 1329 [lxxvi], and a guardianship was assumed by Thomas Randolph, who was then Earl of Moray.

In England, Edward III was determined to avenge the humiliation of England by the Scots. Despite having signed the treaty of Edinburgh-Northampton, Edward III was not the same man as his father. And, though he was young, he had a similarly ambitious nature to that of his grandfather, Edward I. Edward had not acted under his own initiative, having instead been pressured by Roger Mortimer, his regent, as well as his mother, Isabella of France.

The "Peace of Northampton," dubbed by the English as "The shameful peace" had failed to account for reparations to a group of nobles who held land and estates in both England and Scotland. Their properties and titles had been given to Bruce's allies, an act that still sat sourly with both the English nobility and Edward III.

England was suffering from a depleted treasury following the wars waged against Scotland, yet the outraged English people and its king were in no position to attempt any further action against Scotland by themselves.

In 1330, the year following the coronation of David II, saw two events occur which would prove to be significant for both Edward and the future of Scotland. Edward III had his regent; Roger Mortimer, executed, thus taking full control of his crown and country. Secondly, Edward Balliol made an appeal to the now unbridled English king.

The previous king of Scotland, Jon Balliol, who after the English invasion of Scotland in 1296 had been forced to abdicate his throne, had left behind a son; Edward Balliol. Edward Balliol approached the king of England, wanting the return of ancestral lands that he claimed were rightfully his. Before the end of the year, Edward III sent demands to young King David's regent, Thomas Randolph. Randolph delayed responding, despite Edward III pressing the matter with a second request on 22 April 1332. Meanwhile, Balliol and his followers began to prepare for an invasion of Scotland.

The Battle of Dupplin Moor was to be the opening skirmish in what would become known as the Second War of Scottish Independence. The battle was a significant opener to the war, one which was won by Edward Balliol and commander Henry de Beaumont. To circumvent the terms of the Treaty of Northampton, the Scottish rebels and their English allies sailed from several ports in Yorkshire to the Kinghorn in Fife on the 31st of July 1332. [lxxvii] The terms of the Treaty did not permit English forces to cross the Tweed.

From Kinghorn, they eventually marched to Perth. On the 10th of August, the army was camped at Forteviot, a few miles short of the much stronger force led by Donald the Earl of Mar, which was positioned on the heights of Dupplin Moor. A second Scottish force led by Patrick, Earl of Dunbar, was fast approaching Balliol's army from the rear. The predicament lent no courage to the smaller army, and morale in Balliol's camp began to shrink.

Henry Beaumont, the commander of Balliol's army, was accused by the other disinherited lords, claiming he had betrayed them through false promises of Scottish support for Balliol once they had entered Scotland. Beaumont, by far the most experienced soldier on either side, reacted with cool precision, ordering his troops to risk crossing the River Earn at night and launching a surprise attack on the enemy before they could link with the approaching second force.

Overconfident of his superior force, Donald, the Earl of Mar, ordered his army to settle down on the night of 10 August, not bothering to set a watch. At midnight, under the cover of darkness and with no guard present from the opposing army to raise the alarm, Beaumont moved Balliol's force across the Earn to take up a defensive position on high ground at the head of a narrow valley, outflanking Mar.

With the rapid approach of the main Scottish force, Beaumont knew that the time to act was now. The army formed a line, with archers on each flank and men-at-arms at the center, resembling a quarter moon. The Scots, angry that their enemy had outmaneuvered them, charged at the defensively formed English army in disorganized schiltrons, all formation lost to the reckless charge. Mar's wild charge was met with a hail of arrows, falling on the Scottish flanks. The unarmored Scottish footmen, with unvisored helmets, were ill-prepared for the volleys of arrows which fell murderously, thinning their ranks in heartbeats. The superior force, however, was able to get through the storm of arrows and meet the center of the English force, where Beaumont's men-at-arms finally gave some ground. But the unrelenting barrage of arrows thinned out the charging army's flanks, forcing them to push into the middle to escape the rain of death. The larger force lost all ability to maneuver, and the crowded middle ranks of the army were pushed onto the waiting spears of the English.

The Scottish dead were piled high as the battle ended with the English surrounding the mass of bodies. The Scots' losses were heavy; Mar himself was killed as were several other key members of the Scottish army. Estimates of between two and thirteen thousand Scottish dead against relatively light English losses had marked the first battle of the Second War for Scottish Independence, [lxxvii] and not since the battle of Falkirk had the Scottish felt such a terrible defeat. The worst casualty of all was the loss of national confidence that had grown through the successive victories of King Robert Bruce.

Dunbar's army was still in the field, of a similar number to Mar's prior to his defeat. However, the confidence of Balliol and Beaumont's troops soared. The decimation of Mar's troops was felt through the arriving army; Dunbar was reluctant to engage the force that had so thoroughly dispatched one of equal size to his. The English would learn from this battle most keenly, and the formation adopted by Balliol and Beaumont would become a standard battle order, one which would provide England with many future victories.

The decisive victory granted valuable time to Edward Balliol's invasion, also leaving him well-placed in Scotland to gather supporters and swell his ranks. Balliol saw particularly strong support from the residents of Fife and Strathearn. Not long after his victory at Dunbar, Balliol was crowned the King of Scots, a title he used to gain further support as his army marched across the country, eventually settling in Roxburgh.

While at Roxburgh, with his forces swelling due to the spreading news of his victory against the "usurpers" and claim to the throne, Balliol offered his loyalty to Edward III, pledging to support all of Edward's future battles as well as offering to wed David II's sister, a move that would further legitimize his claim to the throne and expand his lands and fortunes. Balliol then left Roxburgh, moving on to Annan, which would be the site of the Camisade of Annan, a battle between the supporters of Balliol and the loyalist troops of David II, led by Sir Archibald Douglas and John Randolph, 3rd Earl of Moray. Balliol would lose this battle to the Bruce Loyalists but manage to escape, fleeing Scotland to return to Edward in England.
[lxxvi]

Meanwhile, David II's own resistance had been thrown into turmoil at the death of Thomas Randolph, his regent. Thomas had been a constant companion to Robert de Bruce in his final years and taken over management of the Bruce's household. Robert had decreed before his death that Randolph would serve as David's regent, a role he performed wisely and with honor before his unfortunate death at Musselburgh. Randolph had been on his way to engage Edward Balliol and his supporters when he died, many believed it to be the result of English poison, but the most likely culprit was a kidney stone.

Edward III invades

Once he had returned to England, Edward Balliol once again offered his loyalty and homage to Edward III, requesting his aid in the combined campaign against Scotland.

Balliol returned to Scotland in March 1333 to lay siege to Berwick-upon-Tweed. Berwick-upon-Tweed held a strategic position on the border between Scotland and England, being the main route for both invasion and trade. The town had a tumultuous past, having been sacked by Edward I in 1296, one of the first actions which marked the beginning of the first Scottish War of Independence. Edward III's justification of the military actions against Berwick-upon-Tweed and the violation of the Treaty of Northampton were due to his claims that Scotland was preparing for war, his incursion being a response to threats from the north.

Balliol crossed the border first with his disinherited Scottish lords on 10 March, accompanied by some English magnates. Edward had invested heavily in the nobles accompanying the campaign, providing grants of over £1,000 to the Englishmen and a similar amount to Balliol and his Scottish nobles. Balliol's army reached Berwick in late March and immediately made moves to encircle the town and cutting off all aid by land, Edward's navy having already done the same by sea.

Edward himself arrived at Berwick with the bulk of the English army on the 9th of May, some six weeks after Balliol had arrived and laid siege. Balliol had not been idle, unleashing a scorched earth policy upon the surrounding lands, ensuring that there was little to no sustenance in the region to resupply the town if the opportunity arose. The town's water supply had already been cut, trenches dug, and all communication out of Berwick was made impossible while Edwards accompanying craftsman began work on the siege engines required to take the town.

A large Scottish army was gathered just north of the border, under the leadership of Sir Archibald Douglas. He concentrated his energy on swelling the ranks of the army rather than utilizing the troops he already had, except for carrying out some minor raiding into Cumberland. Unfortunately, these raids had little effect in drawing the English away from Berwick and instead provided Edward with justification for his military campaign.

By the end of June, with the full support of the English army, its trebuchets and catapults, and also Edward's Navy, Berwick was close to falling. With its garrison exhausted and half the town destroyed, a truce was requested by the defending commander Alexander Seton. Edward agreed to the truce on the condition that Seton surrender by 11 July.

Douglas was now without options, and the army that had gathered north of the border was compelled into action. Douglas had approximately thirteen thousand troops, significantly more than Edward's nine thousand. On the last day of Seton's truce, the army entered England, marching to the port of Tweedmouth. The little port had been destroyed, having been an obstacle for the large Scottish army, who were eager to provide the relief required by the truce set down by Edward.

A few hundred Scottish cavalries were able to navigate their way across the ruins of the old bridge and then force their way to Berwick. In their minds, and in those of the Scottish garrison at

Berwick, the terms of the truce had been satisfied. Edward argued that the relief was to have come from Scotland, or rather the direction of Scotland, while the few hundred Scottish cavalries had entered Berwick from the English side. After much arguing, a fresh truce was agreed to on the provision of relief before the 20th of July.

Douglas knew that a foray against Edward in his current defensive position would be disastrous, even with his superior numbers. To draw the English army out to more favorable terrain, Douglas marched the Scottish army south towards Bamburgh, threatening to besiege the town where Edwards's queen was currently in residence. However, Edward was confident in Bamburgh's defenses, and the Scots had not the time to construct the type of machinery needed to breach the fortress. Instead, the Scottish army ravaged the countryside. Edward ignored this, positioning his army on Halidon Hill, a highly defensive position on a rise of some six hundred feet.

Douglas, out of options, had little choice but to engage Edward on the grounds of his choosing. To engage the English army, the Scots descended downhill to the marshy ground that covered the area before Halidon Hill. Once over the marshy ground they still had the hill to climb before reaching the English forces. The journey left the Scottish spearmen vulnerable to English arrows for a long period of time without cover. Casualties were heavy, however the survivors made it to the crest of the hill, climbing towards the waiting spears of the English. The Scottish army broke; their casualties were in the thousands including Douglas himself. Edwards's casualties were numbered at just fourteen.

The next day Berwick's truce expired, and the town surrendered to Edwards's terms.

The loss of Douglas and the troops at Halidon Hill was a tremendous blow to the supporters of David II. The Scottish king would soon be exiled to France, where he would remain until 1341. Edward Balliol was crowned and quickly fulfilled his promises to Edward. Acknowledging fealty and subjection to the Edward, Balliol surrendered Berwick as an inalienable possession of the English Crown". Following later that year, Balliol also yielded Roxburgh, Edinburgh, Peebles, Dumfries, Linlithgow, and Haddington, [lxxvi] and though Edward did not remove Scottish laws, he did replace the men in charge with his own.

While David II was removed and Edward III attended to the issues of his own kingdom, Balliol was troubled by unrest among both the Scottish nationalists and his own allies. [lxxvi] While Balliol's allies seemed to be deserting him, his enemies were only growing in number. He retired to Berwick, managing to convince Edward III that the situation was under control, though in the meantime more and more of his men were defecting to join those loyal to David II. [lxxvii]

French and English relations were already tense, with Philip VI of France offering shelter to David II. A mutual defensive pact had been signed between Scotland and France in 1295, under the then king Jon Balliol, Edward Balliol's father. After a plea for aid from David's new co-regents, Philip sent an ambassador to England to discuss the recent events between Scotland and England. Unfortunately, not much would be gained by the ambassadors, who; failing to make headway with the disorganized members of David II's loyalist supporters, only succeeded in unwittingly allowing England time to recover their finances. [lxxviii]

In March 1335, having lost confidence in Balliol's ability to hold sway over the Scottish noblemen, Edward began mustering his forces. Scotland was aware of the growing mobilization of English forces and began to quietly prepare. Edward raised his largest army to date, numbering thirteen thousand men, his strategy a three-pronged invasion of Scotland. Balliol would take troops west from Berwick while Edward led his troops north from Carlisle, and a naval force near the Clyde would form the third front of the invasion. The armies encountered little resistance, meeting up at Glasgow and eventually settling in the area of Perth.

In France, an army of six thousand soldiers was openly assembled to aid the Scottish troops. Edward was informed that these troops would be deployed if he did not submit to arbitration by France and the Pope. Edward refused.

Meanwhile, Scottish loyalist forces were not faring well. Andrew Murray agreed to a truce with Edward, lasting from October until Christmas. However, Balliol and his followers were not included in the terms. Balliol, through the support of David III Strathbogie, lay siege against Kildrummy Castle. Murray sent troops after him, routing his force and killing Strathbogie. Balliol would see many more defeats in the coming years that would force him to rely more and more heavily on the English king. [lxxvii]

In May 1336, Edward pushed on with his invasion plans despite the threat from the French. He received reports of the amassing forces of Philip, and intended to block the most likely port of arrival, Aberdeen. Edward moved from Newcastle with a force of four hundred men, swelling his ranks as he marched on Lochindorb, ending Scottish sieges and destroying everything he encountered before burning Aberdeen to the ground.

The English embassy had been attempting to negotiate with Philip VI and David II, however, in August they received final word from Philip; his invasion of England would proceed. French privateers attacked the town of Oxford, also capturing several royal ships. [lxxvi] Edward received word of French actions by September. He abandoned his immediate plans in Scotland and returned to England. However, he was too late to strike back at French ships. He raised funds before returning to Scotland, settling down to winter at the fortress in Clyde after a series of wins and losses. Scotland was under heavy strain, with both English and Scottish forces ravaging the countryside, each trying to eliminate any advantage the other force might acquire. Disease and hunger were rampant among the people.

The Scottish loyalists used the French distractions to their advantage, and by the end of March they had reclaimed most of Scotland north of the Forth and had dealt serious blows to lands owned by Edward Balliol. Edward III was forced to focus on France, vowing to return to Scotland once they had been taken care of. In the meantime, France had also continued to pour supplies into Scotland to aid the Scottish loyalists. The newly provisioned Scottish forces were able to progress further south and into northern England, laying waste to Cumberland and forcing Edward to split his efforts between both French and Scottish threats.

Early winter of 1338 was seen as a turning point for the Scots, and though the ruthless actions of Murray had left such devastation in his own lands that thousands of Scottish people were left without a means to feed themselves, he had effectively ended the possibility for Edward III to establish a stable lordship over southern Scotland. [lxxviii]

Return of the son of the Bruce

David II reached the age of eighteen by the summer of 1341. He returned to Scotland in June of that year, eager to surround himself with his people and begin to establish his own authority. Unfortunately, David made many mistakes, angering some key figures in Scotland's political power base. His authority was undermined by William Douglas, and Robert Stewart swapped the lands they had been given by David. [lxxix]

Skirmishes with the English also continued under David, who conducted several raids into England. In February 1343 the English and French entered into a truce which included Scotland and which was meant to last until September of 1346, through several skirmishes did occur during this time. However, it was not until 1346 that circumstances would change when Philip VI appealed to David II for his support.

Edward II had recently won a dynamic victory in Northern France against Philip at the Battle of Crécy. Philip urged David to invade

England to force Edward to return and deal with the northern threat. David mustered a massive force in Perth, but the English had been given enough time to raise a similar force. On 17 October 1346, both armies met near Durham, to engage in what would become known as the Battle of Neville's cross. The battle would be catastrophic for the Scottish forces, with many of their leaders slain and David II himself taken prisoner.

David would remain a prisoner of the English until 1357, with most of his sentence spent in the Tower of London. [lxxix] With many of the Scottish leadership either slain or taken captive, the future was looking bleak. Edward Balliol wasted no time in gathering combatants to him with the intent to launch an excursion back into Scotland. However, despite Balliol's campaign restoring some of the southern Scottish lands back to Edward III, the campaign on a whole made little headway. Edward's attention had been turned back to France.

Over the next few years, Edward would try to use David and his other captive Sir Archibald Douglas to negotiate favorable terms with Scotland. Edward seemed to lose any interest in securing the interests of Balliol, his negotiations requested David hold Scotland as a fief for England, and named Edward III or one of his sons as successors to the Throne should David not produce an heir. [lxxix] The Scottish lords refused. By 1350 Edward had altered his request, instead ransoming David II for a fee of £40,000, the reinstatement of the disinherited lords, and David's agreement to name Edward's son as his successor should he die without children. The Scots seemed to entertain the idea, requesting time for further negotiation. David II himself was permitted to return to Scotland briefly to aid in the negotiations. However, this offer too would fail, and David would return to England.

Years would pass without any agreement between Edward and Scotland. By 1352 parliament convened to decide upon the fate of David, and Scotland did not find the prospect of Scottish submission to the English as a fair trade for the return of their king.

Edward was still heavily involved in the events in France, and in 1354 offered a simple ransom for the return of David, however, the Scots rejected this as well. In 1355, with French backing, Scottish forces launched a successful campaign against Berwick, reclaiming the town. This would prove a mistake, Edward's retaliation was swift and brutal, invading Scotland in an episode that would become known as the Burnt Candlemas; a military campaign focused not on the engagement of enemy forces but simply the destruction of everything within the army's warpath. Edward recaptured Berwick before moving on to sack Haddington. English armies decimated most of Lothian before burning Edinburgh. [lxxvii]

The Second War of Scottish Independence would end with the Treaty of Berwick, one in which Scotland would agree to pay 100,000 merks to England over a ten-year period. [lxxix] Edward Balliol, weary and ill over decades of war and fighting and with little left to show, would rescind his claim for the Scottish throne in exchange for an annuity of £2000. [lxxvi] David II returned to Scotland, to deal with the political discourse and rivalries common in any court at the time.

The Second War of Scottish Independence demonstrated more so than any other event in the previous hundred years the fruitlessness of a struggle between England and Scotland. Despite the many maneuverings and battles of the period, the two countries were left ultimately in a stalemate, with little gain on either side. Scotland retained some semblance of its independence and England retained its reputation as a leading figure in European powers.

Conclusion

Bruce's death wish (to have his heart be taken on a religious crusade) points towards how his life had pivoted from a personal quest for power to a more symbolic pursuit of a grander, loftier, and more ambiguously defined "Scottish cause." The Scottish nobility may have not been consistent in their support for the right of the Scottish realm to maintain its laws and customs without influence and interference from the English, but it was apparent that the desire for the continued existence of the Kingdom of Scotland had always prevent the Scots from simply submitting themselves to Edward I's overlordship.

William Wallace's rise from being an unknown squire to a war leader and a Guardian of Scotland is a potent symbol for how Scottish men from all walks of life were willing to risk everything in opposing English attempts at conquest. It is certainly worth pointing out that England's ambitions to exert authority over its northern neighbor did not end with Edward I, his son, or his grandson. From the 1290s to Henry IV's reign in 1400, each English king led his own costly attempt to subdue the Scots. Each of these attempts eventually failed.

Edward III, despite being himself a skilled leader akin to his grandfather Edward I, learnt better than most the costs involved in an attempt to subdue the Scots. His own life littered with resentment towards the struggles against the Scottish, his ambition to become overlord of Scotland discarded with the Treaty of Berwick.

The phenomenon of Scottish resistance was nevertheless more complex than a simple "us versus them" scenario. Civil war between the Scottish nobles and local warfare in various towns and counties was part of everyday life through the First Scottish War of Independence. The battles that were fought against the absorption of Scotland into England were nevertheless fought in the name of King John Balliol, who was commonly accepted as the rightful ruler of the realm.

Bruce's bid for the throne in 1306, after the murder of John Comyn, was thus a shocking departure from common expectations. His sacrilegious and criminal action prompted the Scottish supporters of John Balliol and Edward I to unite to oppose him. Bruce's challenge was thus twofold from the very beginning. He had to hold his own ground against the English army on the battlefield *and* to rightfully establish himself as the ruler of Scotland. In time, Bruce decisively demonstrated his military competence by emerging victorious at the Battle of Bannockburn.

Military success alone was nevertheless insufficient for Bruce to mount an undisputed claim for royal rights. Bruce needed the symbolic weight afforded by documents like the Declaration of the Clergy in 1309 and the Declaration of Arbroath in 1320 to support his position as the rightful king of the community. Bruce attempted to discredit Balliol's claim to the throne by advancing the argument that a king who submitted to England had forfeited his rights. Bruce's propaganda aimed to establish himself as the rightful defender of the realm who could defend its freedom against the formidable English army.

Given his precarious standing, Bruce was always paranoid about the possibility of being undermined and displaced. The enemies he had exiled – chiefly Edward Balliol[lxix] – were biding their time, waiting for the right moment to strike. Bruce also had to contend with Scottish nobles and magnates who were fatigued by the constant warfare Scotland had to endure under Bruce's command. Within a few months after the Declaration of Arbroath, Bruce had to contend with the unsuccessful conspiracy of 1320. Its aim was to replace him with Balliol and establish a peaceful truce with England. Bruce was also troubled by his lack of a suitable adult heir that could take his place. To better ensure that the Scottish nobility would support the authority of the Bruce family, he carefully promoted and enhanced the standings of his supporters. The magnates who opposed him found their lands and titles redistributed to Bruce's supporters – who were encouraged to cultivate a personal stake in the survival of the Bruce royal line.

The Treaty of Edinburgh-Northampton initially appeared to achieve everything that Bruce had fought for. The English had withdrawn their claims of overlordship. Scotland was finally at peace, and Bruce finally had a male heir to continue his hard-won royal line. And yet, a mere three years after Bruce's death, Scotland was in turmoil once again. In 1332, Edward Balliol - the son of the king that the majority of Scots had accepted before Bruce's unexpected campaign for the throne – led an invasion of Scotland. He was supported by a group of English nobles whose lands in Scotland had been seized and redistributed by Robert Bruce. Despite their larger numbers, the army led by Donald, Earl of Mar and regent for David II[lxx] (who was then eight years old) was defeated at Dupplin Moor (near Perth). Edward Balliol was then crowned king at Scone. A new civil war between the Balliol supporters and Bruce supporters had been triggered.

Seeing the opportunity to restore England's might during the reign of his grandfather, Edward III denounced the peace that Isabella and Mortimer had brokered with Robert Bruce in 1328 as being "shameful." Despite being only 14 when he had been heavily persuaded by his mother and Roger Mortimer to sign it, he had been deeply troubled by the treaty. Not long after his marriage to Philippa at York, he established his independence and position as England's ruler. In 1330, he snuck into a Nottingham castle where a council was held and took Mortimer prisoner.

Mortimer was swiftly executed. As Isabella's paramour, Mortimer had thoroughly abused his position as the most powerful man in England. He had acquired the lordships of Denbigh, Oswestry, and

Clun for himself, and received additional lordships from the queen. His greed, arrogance, and unpopular policy instigated deep hostility from the barons. Henry of Lancaster thus helped the young king to capture Mortimer, condemn him for his crimes, and hang him as a traitor. His enormous estates were then forfeited to the crown. Edward III respected his mother and forgave her for the illicit liaison, but did not hesitate to end her political influence. Forced into retirement, Isabella eventually joined the Poor Clares, an order of nuns, in her later years.

Edward III took advantage of David II's young age to help the exiled Scottish barons restore Edward Balliol to the Scottish throne. In return, Balliol would recognize Edward III's overlordship and ordered for the cession of southern Southland. This earned Balliol widespread resentment for being a puppet of an English king. On December 1332, a Scottish resistance force led by Sir Archibald Douglas defeated Balliol at Annan, Dumfries. With Edward III's help, Balliol was able to defeat and kill Douglas during a second confrontation at Halidon (on the outskirts of Berwick) in July the following year. He thus cemented an uncertain authority over the majority of Scotland.

David II was forced to flee to France in 1334 to ensure his own safety. He was received warmly by King Philip VI. In 1339 and 1340, he assisted the French king in his unproductive campaigns against Edward III. Like his father, David II eventually returned to regain his authority over Scotland. England's ambition for conquest was thwarted once again. With the help of experienced local captains and guardians, the Bruce faction was able to defeat Balliol's forces and the English garrisons. David II returned to Scotland as King in 1341, in control of a majority of the realm.

Inspired to emulate his father's military accomplishments, David II embarked on a series of ultimately unsuccessful invasions of northern England. His efforts culminated in the ambitious battle at Neville's Cross outside Durham in 1346. His army was defeated and David II himself was captured by the English. If Robert Bruce had been captured by the English during his campaigns, Scotland's quest for independence would have certainly been doomed. By this time, however, Edward III's zeal to establish an overlordship over Scotland had waned. He did mount a final invasion in 1356, but there was no great effort to subjugate Scotland within the intervening decade. Instead, the conflict between the English and Scottish were confined to small battles over Scottish border communities and control of surviving English strongholds in Scotland. In 1409, only Roxburgh and Berwick remained under English control.

England may have been the wealthier and more powerful nation, but its leaders were unable to convert their military successes into a final and unrelenting victory. Despite winning control of key Scottish strongholds and maintaining the presence of the English army in various Scottish territories, undisputed control of Scotland proved to be highly elusive (particularly in the western and northern regions). There was also the problem of limited resources. Edward I's attempts were most successful because he had the luxury of making the Scottish conquest the sole focus of his attention during the early 1300s and mid-1330s. His successors had to divide their attention between domestic conflicts and continental wars; for example, Edward III's Hundred Years' War with France, which unfolded between 1337 and 1453.[lxxi] (Given France's history of providing refuge to David II and its support for the Scots during Edward III's attempts at conquest, it was natural for David II to (unsuccessfully) invade England in 1346 in return).

By 1356, Edward Balliol had given up hope of reclaiming the Scottish throne for himself. He resigned his titles and relinquished all his lands to Edward III in January that year. He would die without leaving behind any heir, ending the Balliol line's claim to the throne. After being held an English prisoner for a decade, David II was released in 1357 in return for a hefty ransom. In his absence, Robert Stewart (his nephew and heir) and William Douglas had been defending and leading the realm.

David II's attempts to expand his royal power, wealth and influence – despite being burdened by the ransom he owed to England III – alienated Stewart and Douglas. He also attempted to allow Edward III's son to succeed the Scottish throne in exchange for his impossible ransom to be repaid (he did not have any heir to succeed him). Many found this proposition unthinkable – especially Stewart, who was the rightful successor to the throne. David II and his knights had to quash the rebellion organized by Stewart and Douglas. In the end, the Scottish parliament repudiated the idea of an English succession. In his final years, David II inspired additional political opposition for his financial extravagance.

After his death in early 1371, Robert II[lxxii] assumed the throne of Scotland as the first Stewart sovereign. Being the maternal grandson of Robert Bruce, he had been Scotland's presumptive heir for the majority of his fifty-four years. He aimed to consolidate his wealth and power to ensure that the throne remained with the Stewart lineage. By furthering the mutual interests of his extended family, he was able to engender a climate of political stability in the 1370s. By 1384, however, internal rivalries would disrupt the peace. Robert II was usurped by his own heir and eldest son, John Earl of Carrick. In 1388, Carrick himself was displaced by his own younger brother, Robert of Fife.

These were not simply toxic family rivalries for ultimate power. They were also a reflection of the failure of the monarchy and its lieutenants to maintain the stability of the kingdom's regional communities – a task that had been made considerably more complex by the long years of war with England. The Southern magnates demanded support and assistance in attempts to combat the English. Meanwhile, there were concerns that the magnates of the Highlands were impinging on the rights and interests of their Lowland counterparts. Dissatisfied with the inability of the monarch to protect their interests, Scotland became more dominated by regionalized politics from 1388 onward. The distinction between the king himself and his chief subjects – who might be elevated for the purposes of political or military expedience – had been blurred.

Despite these problems, the Scottish crown remained independent from England until 1603. After the death of Elizabeth I, James VI of Scotland ascended to the English throne and became James I. This marked the first time where England and Scotland were ruled by a single monarch. This tradition would continue until 1707, when the Act of Union was signed. This treaty meant that England and Scotland would be united as Great Britain.[lxxiii] It established peace, open borders and prosperity between both lands in a way that William Wallace and Robert Bruce would probably have never imagined. And yet, Scottish culture flourished and retained its own distinct identity. This was partly due to the separation of the court system and the church – a consequence of Wallace and Bruce's long and difficult struggle for an identity to call their own.[lxxiv] Their battles and deeds live on in Scotland's national myths, instilling pride in the nation's separate identity and existence. Each generation extolls the battles these national heroes won and lost, in their valiant efforts to ensure the continuity of crown, community of the realm, and nation.

Here's is another book by Captivating History that we think you would be interested in!

WILLIAM WALLACE

UNA GUÍA FASCINANTE SOBRE UN COMBATIENTE DE LA LIBERTAD Y MÁRTIR QUE MARCÓ LA HISTORIA E INDEPENDENCIA DE ESCOCIA DE INGLATERRA

CAPTIVATING HISTORY

Check out this book!

References

[i] "Edward I: King of England." *Encyclopedia Britannica.* https://www.britannica.com/biography/Edward-I-king-of-England. Accessed 15 June 2018.

[ii] "Battle of Falkirk." *Encyclopedia Britannica.* https://www.britannica.com/topic/battle-of-Falkirk. Accessed 15 March 2018.

[iii] Ibid.

[iv] "Boniface VIII: Pope." *Encyclopedia Britannica.* https://www.britannica.com/biography/Boniface-VIII. Accessed 15 June 2018.

[v] "John Comyn: Scottish leader." *Encyclopedia Britannica.* https://www.britannica.com/biography/John-Comyn. Accessed 15 June 2018.

[vi] "Edward II: King of England." *Encyclopedia Britannica.* https://www.britannica.com/biography/Edward-II-king-of-England. Accessed 15 June 2018.

[vii] "Battle of Stirling Bridge." *Encyclopedia Britannica.* http://www.bbc.co.uk/scotland/history/articles/battle_of_stirling_bridge/. Accessed 15 June 2018.

[viii] "Battle of Bannockburn." *Encyclopedia Britannica.* https://www.britannica.com/event/Battle-of-Bannockburn. Accessed 15 June 2018.

[ix] "Alexander III: King of Scotland." *Encyclopedia Britannica.* https://www.britannica.com/biography/Alexander-III-king-of-Scotland. Accessed 15 June 2018.

[x] Wormald, Jenny. *Scotland: A History.* 2005.

[xi] Ibid.

[xii] "Berwick." *Encyclopedia Britannica.* https://www.britannica.com/place/Berwickshire. Accessed 15 June 2018.

[xiii] "Glasgow." *Encyclopedia Britannica.* https://www.britannica.com/place/Glasgow-Scotland. Accessed 15 June 2018.

[xiv] "Edinburgh." *Encyclopedia Britannica.* https://www.britannica.com/place/Edinburgh-Scotland. Accessed 15 June 2018.

[xv] "David I: King of Scotland." *Encyclopedia Britannica.* https://www.britannica.com/biography/David-I. Accessed 15 June 2018.

[xvi] Penman, Michael. *Robert the Bruce: King of the Scots.* 2014.

[xvii] Wormald, Jenny. *Scotland: A History.* 2005.

[xviii] "William I: King of England." *Encyclopedia Britannica.* https://www.britannica.com/biography/William-I-king-of-England. Accessed 15 June 2018.

[xix] "Treaty of Falaise." *Encyclopedia Britannica.* https://www.britannica.com/topic/Treaty-of-Falaise. Accessed 15 June 2018.

[xx] "Richard I: King of England." https://www.britannica.com/biography/Richard-I-king-of-England. Accessed 15 June 2018.

[xxi] "Philip IV: King of France." *Encyclopedia Britannica.* https://www.britannica.com/biography/Philip-IV-king-of-France. Accessed 15 June 2018.

[xxii] "Thomas the Rhymer." *Encyclopedia Britannica.* https://www.britannica.com/biography/Thomas-the-Rhymer. Accessed 15 June 2018.

[xxiii] "Margaret: Queen of Scotland." *Encyclopedia Britannica.* https://www.britannica.com/biography/Margaret-queen-of-Scotland. Accessed 15 June 2018.

[xxiv] "Erik II: King of Norway." *Encyclopedia Britannica.* https://www.britannica.com/biography/Erik-II. Accessed 15 June 2018.

[xxv] "The Treaty of Birgham." http://www.bbc.co.uk/bitesize/higher/history/warsofindependence/thegreatcause/revision/2/. Accessed 15 June 2018.

[xxvi] Wormald, Jenny. *Scotland: A History.* 2005.

[xxvii] "John de Balliol: Scottish magnate." *Encyclopedia Britannica.* https://www.britannica.com/biography/John-de-Balliol. Accessed 15 June 2018.

[xxviii] "Robert de Bruce: King of Scotland." *Encyclopedia Britannica.* https://www.britannica.com/biography/Robert-the-Bruce. Accessed 15 June 2018.

[xxix] "Henry III: King of England [1207 – 1272]." *Encyclopedia Britannica.* https://www.britannica.com/biography/Henry-III-king-of-England-1207-1272. Accessed 15 June 2018.

[xxx] Rhymer, Thomas. *Foedera II.* 1745.

[xxxi] "William Wallace." *BBC.* http://www.bbc.co.uk/scotland/history/articles/william_wallace/. Accessed 15 June 2018.

[xxxii] "Braveheart: Film by Gibson [1995]." *Encyclopedia Britannica.* https://www.britannica.com/topic/Braveheart. Accessed 15 June 2018.

[xxxiii] "Harry the Minstrel: Scottish writer." *Encyclopedia Britannica.* https://www.britannica.com/biography/Harry-the-Minstrel. Accessed 15 June 2018.

[xxxiv] Hamilton, William and Elspeth King. *Blind Harry's Wallace.* 2003.

[xxxv] McKay, James. *William Wallace: Brave Heart.* 1995.

[xxxvi] Murison, A.F. *Famous Scots: Sir William Wallace.* 1898.

[xxxvii] "Robert the Bruce." *Encyclopedia Britannica.* https://www.britannica.com/biography/Robert-the-Bruce. Accessed 15 June 2018.

[xxxviii] "John de Warenne, 6th earl of Surrey." *Encyclopedia Britannica.* https://www.britannica.com/biography/John-de-Warenne-6th-earl-of-Surrey. Accessed 15 June 2018.

[xxxix] "Edward I: King of England." *Encyclopedia Britannica.* https://www.britannica.com/biography/Edward-I-king-of-England. Accessed 15 June 2018.

[xl] "Drawing and quartering." *Encyclopedia Britannica.* https://www.britannica.com/topic/drawing-and-quartering. Accessed 15 June 2018.

[xli] "Jasper Tudor, duke of Bedford: Welsh noble." *Encyclopedia Britannica.* https://www.britannica.com/biography/Jasper-Tudor-duke-of-Bedford. Accessed 15 June 2018.

[xlii] Penman, Michael. *Robert the Bruce: King of the Scots.* 2014.

[xliii] "Robert the Bruce, King of Scots 1306 – 1329." *BBC.* http://www.bbc.co.uk/scotland/history/articles/robert_the_bruce/. Accessed 15 June 2018.

[xliv] "War of Independence." *BBC*. http://www.bbc.co.uk/scotland/education/as/warsofindependence/info.shtml?loc=stone. Accessed 15 June 2018.

[xlv] "Piers Gaveston, earl of Cornwall." *Encyclopedia Britannica*. https://www.britannica.com/biography/Piers-Gaveston-Earl-of-Cornwall. Accessed 15 June 2018.

[xlvi] "Isabella of France." *Encyclopedia Britannica*. https://www.britannica.com/biography/Isabella-of-France. Accessed 15 June 2018.

[xlvii] "Menage a Roi: Edward II and Piers Gaveston." *History Today*. https://www.historytoday.com/js-hamilton/menage-roi-edward-ii-and-piers-gaveston. Accessed 15 June 2018.

[xlviii] "Piers Gaveston: bending the monarch's ear, and will." *The Telegraph*. https://www.telegraph.co.uk/history/9264564/Piers-Gaveston-bending-the-monarchs-ear-and-will.html. Accessed 15 June 2018.

[xlix] "Pike." *Encyclopedia Britannica*. https://www.britannica.com/topic/Ordinances. Accessed 15 June 2018.

[l] "Despenser family." *Encyclopedia Britannica*. https://www.britannica.com/topic/Despenser-family. Accessed 15 June 2018.

[li] Penman, Michael. *Robert the Bruce: King of the Scots*. 2014.

[lii] Wormald, Jenny. *Scotland: A History*. 2005.

[liii] "The Battle of Bannockburn, 1314." *BBC*. http://www.bbc.co.uk/scotland/history/articles/battle_of_bannockburn/. Accessed 15 June 2018.

[liv] "Ordinances: English history." *Encyclopedia Britannica*. https://www.britannica.com/technology/pike-weapon. Accessed 15 June 2018.

[lv] "Thomas Randolph, 1st earl of Moray." *Encyclopedia Britannica*. https://www.britannica.com/biography/Thomas-Randolph-1st-Earl-of-Moray. Accessed 15 June 2018.

[lvi] "Bannockburn Factsheet (II)." *BBC*. http://www.bbc.co.uk/history/scottishhistory/independence/trails_independence_bannockburn2.shtml. Accessed 15 June 2018.

[lvii] "The Battle of Bannockburn, 1314." *BBC*. http://www.bbc.co.uk/scotland/history/articles/battle_of_bannockburn/. Accessed 15 June 2018.

[lviii] "Battle of the Golden Spurs." *Encyclopedia Britannica.* https://www.britannica.com/event/Battle-of-the-Golden-Spurs. Accessed 15 June 2018.

[lix] "War of The Three Kings: Scotland's invasion of Ireland." *Encyclopedia Britannica.* https://www.bbc.com/news/uk-northern-ireland-33913315. Accessed 15 June 2018.

[lx] "Thomas Randolph, 1st earl of Moray." *Encyclopedia Britannica.* https://www.britannica.com/biography/Thomas-Randolph-1st-Earl-of-Moray. Accessed 15 June 2018.

[lxi] "Sir James Douglas." *Encyclopedia Britannica.* https://www.britannica.com/biography/James-Douglas-Scottish-noble. Accessed 15 June 2018.

[lxii] "John XXII: Pope." *Encyclopedia Britannica.* https://www.britannica.com/biography/John-XXII. Accessed 15 June 2018.

[lxiii] "Charles IV: King of France." *Encyclopedia Britannica.* https://www.britannica.com/biography/Charles-IV-king-of-France. Accessed 15 June 2018.

[lxiv] "Roger Mortimer, 1st earl of March: English noble." *Encyclopedia Britannica.* https://www.britannica.com/biography/Roger-Mortimer-1st-Earl-of-March. Accessed 15 June 2018.

[lxv] "Edward III." *Encyclopedia Britannica.* https://www.britannica.com/biography/Edward-III-king-of-England. Accessed 15 June 2018.

[lxvi] "Treaty of Northampton." *Encyclopedia Britannica.* https://www.britannica.com/topic/Treaty-of-Northampton. Accessed 15 June 2018.

[lxvii] "John Barbour." *Encyclopedia Britannica.* https://www.britannica.com/biography/John-Barbour. Accessed 15 June 2018.

[lxviii] "Robert the Bruce's heart finds its final resting place." *The Independent.* https://www.independent.co.uk/news/robert-the-bruces-heart-finds-its-final-resting-place-1167359.html. Accessed 15 June 2018.

[lxix] "Edward: King of Scotland." *Encyclopedia Britannica.* https://www.britannica.com/biography/Edward-king-of-Scotland. Accessed 15 June 2018.

[lxx] "David II: King of Scotland." *Encyclopedia Britannica.* https://www.britannica.com/biography/David-II. Accessed 15 June 2018.

[lxxi] "Hundred Years' War." *Encyclopedia Britannica.* https://www.britannica.com/event/Hundred-Years-War. Accessed 15 June 2018.

[lxxii] "Robert II: King of Scotland." *Encyclopedia Britannica.* https://www.britannica.com/biography/Robert-II-king-of-Scotland. Accessed 15 June 2018.

[lxxiii] "Act of Union." *Encyclopedia Britannica.* https://www.britannica.com/event/Act-of-Union-Great-Britain-1707. Accessed 15 June 2018.

[lxxiv] "Book Review: 'Robert the Bruce' by Michael Penman; 'Bannockburn' by Angus Konstam; 'Bannockburns' by Robert Crawford." *Wall Street Journal.* https://www.wsj.com/articles/book-review-robert-the-bruce-by-michael-penman-bannockburn-by-angus-konstam-bannockburns-by-robert-crawford-1410556022. Accessed 15 June 2018.

[lxxvi] Lang, Andrew *(1903). A history of Scotland from the Roman occupation. Dodd, Mead and Co.* Retrieved 25 June 2018.

[lxxvii] Brown, Michael *(28 July 2004). The wars of Scotland, 1214-1371.* Edinburgh University Press. Retrieved 25 June 2018.

[lxxviii] Sumption, Jonathan *(1999). The Hundred Years War: Trial by battle.* University of Pennsylvania Press. Retrieved 25 June 2018.

[lxxix] *Webster, Bruce (2004).* "David II (1324–1371)". *Oxford Dictionary of National Biography. Oxford University Press.* doi:10.1093/ref:odnb/3726. Retrieved 25 June 2018.

Printed in Great Britain
by Amazon